MOVING BEYOND MONEY

How we Overcame Underearning

A FINANCIAL RECOVERY BOOK

MOVING BEYOND MONEY

How we Overcame Underearning

A FINANCIAL RECOVERY BOOK
IN SERVICE TO UNDEREARNERS ANONYMOUS

COPYRIGHT 2021

Library of Congress Cataloging In Publication Data

Batya in Ohio and G in Tennessee, EDS.

Moving Beyond Money : How We Overcame Underearning.

-1st *ed.*

ISBN -13 978-0-578-91345-2

1. *Recovery-Twelve Step Recovery- Self Help 2. Counseling-Financial Therapy 3. Addiction Recovery*

Book Design By: Zenzilé's Way Consulting

Printed In USA

Dedication:

This book is dedicated to the people who helped us overcome our underearning, our sponsors, action group members, action partners and the founders of Underearners Anonymous.

This book is also dedicated to those who still suffer from the diseases of debting, underbeing and underearning.

A note from the editors:

Between the two of us, we have over a decade of financial recovery. We met in a special interest recovery meeting and have worked together on various writing projects, as support persons and through weekly goal and action groups.

We have experienced tremendous financial recovery including being relieved of fear and emotional pain, doubling our incomes, multiplying our income streams, procuring new employment, improving our personal relationships, and even acquiring new property! We have begun to glimpse how jobs can become places of joyful earning and healthy relationships instead of sites of resentment and frustration, as we learn to take the problems of any workplace less personally.

We have learned the joys of being more visible, advocating for ourselves, acquiring new vehicles, accomplishing steps towards enacting our visions, giving back to our various communities, and increasing self-care as we dealt with childhood issues and relaxed into becoming human beings rather than functioning all the time as humans doing. Most importantly, we have had the spiritual experience that all recovery aims for and developed our personal visions of spiritual prosperity. We are closing the "god sized" hole, and becoming right sized, while we pursue our goals and dreams on solid footing. Finally, we have learned to use the principles of recovery, not just for money and finances, but in ALL our affairs.

***

The specific idea of this book began to emerge as I (B) was turning my deep-seated fears about money over to a sponsor in UA five years into my program process. He was sharing his experiences so very generously with me every time I shared mine, that somewhere in the middle of these conversations, I began to come out of the years of shame about money I had been pressing so far down that I had scarcely even been aware of what kind of monsters had been thrashing and swimming around, bumping into each other down there. By sharing his personal anecdotes, one by one, each time I revealed something horrible about my past, he had normalized my experiences and given me the gift of feeling that truly, I was not alone in all of this. Although we were of different ages and genders and had grown up in far-flung parts of the country, we shared an ethnicity that allowed us to resonate deeply even though physically we had never met. The frame he provided to support me allowed me to come to rest at last, metaphorically, on a solid mattress and a very supportive bed, after tossing and turning fitfully and never getting a good night's rest for years on end instead.

Only after hearing his stories was I able to shed my shame, like throwing a dirty dank blanket off the bed that had been weighing heavily. Once I threw off the shame, I was ready to see how I had been acting out, financially, hurting others as well as myself over the years.

Somewhere along the journey of this process, I said I wanted to write a money book, by collecting stories about how people's feelings about money had changed as they worked the steps. He said there was already a book like that in DA, called *Currency of Hope*. I ordered a copy immediately. I read a bit daily, again experiencing a liberatory process.

When it came time for me to think how to give back to the community in Step 12, as a form of service, I knew it was time for *The Money Book* to come to be, although now it has a more elegant title, thanks to my co-editor G.

Many of us have been connecting in many rooms, fellowships, sisterhoods, houses, and programs, through various mediums and means, but some things have not changed, notably, the principles that happiness, joy, and freedom can seldom be arrived at unless we are willing to dive in to, examine, and even re-experience, return from, and share our deepest pain. For many of us, this has led to spiritual awareness.

So, no matter where any reader is, or how far along each of us may have come in the process, something is to be gained by recognizing resonances of one's own personal difficulties, struggles and achievements. As each reader discovers a line, a moment, or a phrase, reading of someone else's experiences might just serve as that medicinal capsule able to bring about an energetic shift allowing for a release of pain.

We thank each of our generous contributors for the ability to bear witness, and we express our deepest gratitude for each who was willing to serve. Each who chose to sit down and write a chapter has, like a sponsor, committed to creation of a channel of empathy for a reader who, like a sponsee, will benefit equally by the share. We hope and pray that each and every reader is able to benefit from this project.

--B, 2019

When I (G) came into Underearners Anonymous, it was as a person new to twelve step programs overall, and especially new to financial recovery. Everyone remarked about how young the fellowship was yet consistently marveled at how the program had up leveled not only their financial lives, but their recovery overall. I heard statements like, "Underearners Anonymous is the PhD of all recovery programs," or that this was the program that really made people take a new look at their previous programs. I was timid and full of trepidation, but somehow found enough evidence to trust that this program would support me in my own desperately sought recovery as well.

My recovery taught me surprising things about myself and how I interacted in the world. For example, I had been a stellar student my entire career, winning many awards and scholarships, yet, when facing my feelings of inadequacy, I found out much more about the reality of my UA symptom of "Hiding and Biting." In the process of compiling this text, I was able to witness other fellow's recovery, how they built community in recovery through outreach, sharing their experience, strength, and hope. In connecting with our fellows, through writing, we also witnessed the relief they felt in the process of writing their own stories, the gratitude of looking at their experiences and the newfound vistas of future recovery.

B and I also expanded our own recovery in compiling this anthology. We truly had an opportunity to practice the twelfth step of taking recovery to the underearner who still suffered. We were able to do deep, lasting, and meaningful service, and we strengthened our own relationship as action group partners and fellow travelers. Combining our very similar yet widely differing academic backgrounds, we began to operate from a place of true strength as professionals and recovery peers. This, we gather, is the true goal of recovery, working well with others to offer our gifts and talents to the world without the drama and trauma of addictive behaviors. In the years since we joined the fellowship, UA has matured, and as a part of that we are happy to present this offering for future fellows in and out of recovery as they journey into their own new way of being, of shining and showing up in the world. We believe that in completing this work, we have built a legacy for future seekers of financial recovery and truly accomplished the goals of the founders and ourselves.

--G, 2021

Table of Contents

PART ONE

Introduction

Chapter One

From Self Help to Twelve Steps

G from Tennessee

When I (G) entered financial recovery, it was only after using every option I could think of to earn, to "fix myself" and to learn as much as I could about money. I often preface my recovery story by saying I own a self-help book for every symptom of what I later learned was the disease of underbeing and underearning… I had briefly heard of this idea of "under"-something as a child… I grew up in the era of Bart Simpson and he was America's beloved bad-boy underachiever. I knew I was the opposite… I overachieved! Earning awards to prove it along the way. I had collected a trail of awards from organizations large and small, from academic, civic, and social organizations. I was zealous and relentless. By the time I made it to recovery, I had collected multiple degrees, certifications, and accolades, only to find myself still broke and largely broken. The over-achieving meant that my identity was so tied to accomplishments, that there was no room for me to just "be." Although I had collected a certification in Yoga and Pranayama, Healing Touch Therapy and studied a few other healing modalities, I had not yet learned to simply BE.

1. Getting to Program

Considering my level of fragility, it was a true miracle and act of God that got me into recovery… I was listening to a business podcast (again!!!) when a woman named Barbara Huson (neé Stanny) talked about her book Overcoming Underearning. It was for highly skilled women who weren't earning to match their credentials or potential. I knew it! This book was for me! I ordered it immediately on amazon, used, and fortunately received a pristine copy that the previous owner had clearly only slightly used. Ms. Huson's book had a 30-day plan, and I read and followed it as closely as I could. I ran into a lot of fear and internal blocks. However, I did find solace in knowing I did have some of the tasks under my belt. The plot twist? At the end of the book she stated, if you aren't doing better after completing these tasks, get into recovery! Which I promptly did. When I joined my first meeting, I felt saved. I knew immediately I was in the right place… Suddenly I heard a list of symptoms, which sounded like the complaints my own parents had about me growing up. I was also filled with resentment… Why hadn't my parents helped me with these problems instead of just criticizing me? Then the embarrassment and shame set in… oh no, I'm broken… my parents knew it and didn't try to fix me… everyone must have known it, and they all just let me move right along!? Finally, I was grateful. I was SO happy that I now had access to what I needed to be a functional, healthy, and balanced adult. I resolved to spend at least 4 years in program which equated to 10% of my life at that point, as I was nearing 40. I figured four years of doing the "right" things could give me some sort of reprieve from all the ways I had been "wrong" out in the world.

2. My Program Experience

I'm a researcher by nature and by trade, so when I began attending my financial recovery program, I scoured the website. I found out about meetings, downloaded program literature, and printed out the symptoms, the steps, the tools, and the traditions. I attended my meeting well prepared, and completely afraid. After hearing the same information that I printed out being read at a meeting, I felt confident that this was "real"... real in the sense that the financial recovery I sought was being experienced by others, real in the sense that there were others like me and a place we could actually get help, and real in the sense that this wasn't just another coaching program or webinar to sell me some high priced service that I definitely couldn't afford. Satisfied, I attended another meeting the next night. That night I introduced myself as a newcomer, and after discussing my symptoms, I was directed to another meeting that addressed exactly what I was facing. This meeting became my home meeting, and I attended religiously for the next 90 days, competing a "90 in 90."

At the end of that time, I had to admit I was starting to feel better and call out my behaviors… I had gained awareness, but I was a long way from recovery. After completing my 90 in 90, I continued doing service, offering to read, and greet newcomers, while keeping up a schedule of sharing at least 3 times a week. I knew being visible on the lines and actively seeking sponsorship were key to me getting the real benefits of program. After nearly a year and a half in program, my sponsor found me. In this time, I had upped my meeting attendance to twice daily, once in the morning to get myself in alignment mentally, and once at the end of the day to find relief from the tension of resisting my compulsive behaviors all day.

I had also connected with an action partner, a program person I worked with daily to share and affirm recovery actions that I would take daily. Finally, I connected with a group of people in my financial recovery program who shared my vocation. We had a small meeting weekly in order to share our experience, strength, and hope as well as to get what I call "safe, sane and sober" actions to take over the next week to maintain our recovery.

Working with people in these ways prepared me for the intense work of working with a sponsor as we read through the Big Book and took the steps. Completing my step work helped me heal from and recognize the buried guilt, shame, and anger I had been living with. It caused me to face, for once and for all, the real issues I faced in my life. The patterns of behavior I engaged in which had to be stopped… not through force of will, or training, but by handing my life over to a power greater than myself, and asking for a reprieve from them daily, while taking actions to move forward in a new, recovered manner.

The road to recovery is seldom a clear path. Every person in program, therapy, or any other form of healing faces obstacles and "life's vicissitudes" I was no different than the hundreds of thousands of others. After securing a position that paid more than I ever earned, my unrecovered self-came head-to-head with an incredibly manipulative and abusive "boss." Like many in recovery, I held severe resentment for authority figures, and this employment situation was the perfect storm for a disaster.

The first red flag was a lack of boundaries, as this was an independent contractor position. I failed to communicate my boundaries around work, and the person I worked for assumed that because she was always "on" the entire team should be "on" too. We were often met with text messages and emails at the crack of dawn, demanding certain tasks be completed or that we be present at an impromptu meeting. A natural go-getter, once I had a target, I was ready to execute. However, the lack of communication I experienced led to a lot of hurt feelings and verbal reprimands when things weren't done to her exact specifications. Needless to say, after "taking" so much and not asking for what I needed, my frustration got the best of me, and I acted out on a business trip. I vented to my co-workers about the obvious abuse of the boss and demanded we all as a team stand up for ourselves. This backfired significantly when one of my coworkers, a woman who was also abused by this woman, repeated everything I said, word for word, to our boss. I was reprimanded, and subsequently fired via a dismissive email.

Once again, I was at a new bottom. I firmly believed that this was the fault of this abusive and manipulative woman. After completing my fourth step inventory I quickly realized I had a pattern of "staying too long" a habit ingrained in my childhood—"do your best, be thorough, do everything YOU can to succeed." I also learned that I had a practice of perfectionism courtesy of another childhood refrain, "you're a Black woman, you have to be twice as good to get half as far." This meant that I not only expected myself and my work to be as perfect as possible, I had the same expectation of the people I worked for and with. Finally, I learned I had that pesky habit of, as we say in recovery, "searching for oranges at the hardware store," I expected this woman to do things she simply wasn't capable of. I failed to notice that this company had a ridiculously high turnover rate, with a brand-new staff every year and that every departure was like a covert escape. I stayed for the money, even though the environment was toxic and demeaning. Ultimately this meant I faced a question of self-love—why would I allow myself to be treated so poorly? Thankfully, recovery has helped me to see the error of my ways, relate to people peer-to-peer versus as an inferior full of fear, and finally love myself and be brave enough to get out of situations that do not serve me.

After leaving this position, I was determined that my next work experience would be better… I spent a great deal of time promoting my own business and was able to keep the lights on while working for myself. I also started applying for jobs, and much to my chagrin, nothing panned out. Finally, I gave my work situation over to my Higher Power, and just began to be grateful in advance for the opportunities I did have. This shift in mindset along with a commitment to continue my recovery work no matter what, eventually led to a breakthrough in work. While working in a part time highly contingent job, I was offered a long-term appointment, full time with pay and benefits. This experience was truly a testament to my consistency and my higher power's ability to work miracles on my behalf.

Doing the work of recovery helped me to create a vision for my life. It showed me a new way to live. I had a newfound sense of gratitude. I had real financial recovery which included being able to do the work I was trained to do, as well as earn more while doing it. I stopped abusing money, and developed a healthy relationship with money, myself, and my higher power. In fact, I had a newfound higher power. One who was expansive, abundant, loving, spoke gently to me, and was out to conspire for my success, instead of punish and penalize. I learned to be gentler with myself, while setting my boundaries for others. I gained --through divine downloads-- new topline and bottom-line behaviors with my finances, and I'm still receiving the bounty of recovery as I use more of the tools, connect to more fellows, and do the service of sponsorship.

3. Why this book?

For those familiar with the world of recovery, getting into program, working the steps, and experiencing the results often becomes a way of life. In fact, in the 12th step, we actively commit to "practicing these principles in all our affairs." However, for the newcomer, a person completely unaware of program, or those who know nothing about the steps, program can be an overwhelming space and somewhat intimidating, as we seek out solutions to lifelong challenges while attempting to trust strangers whom we know nothing about... outside of their program experience.

This book is for the newbie. It is for the person who is in pain, anxiety and fear every day about their financial life. It is for people who are new to program, recovery, or even financial literacy in general. It is for those who are in awe of the idea that working with strangers to get better is possible. It is for individuals with the natural trepidation about a system (the 12-step program) that is often largely unknown, requires anonymity yet demands transparency for healing and recovery. It is for those who have tried "everything else" and found that nothing has worked. Program is a place where "working with others" never fails. For those who have engaged in compulsive behaviors, or who are addicted to behaviors that are damaging--sending them on emotional highs and lows, working with others who have a daily reprieve from their compulsions and addictions supports us in remaining compulsion and addiction free. This book is to remind newcomers of this promise. That getting into program and working with others will be the key to their own daily reprieve.

I am convinced that this book will be useful, as it was through a book that I found my own recovery program. It was lifesaving, as I later found my fellowship had no meetings in my area, or even in my city. No one even had a name for what I was experiencing. The fear, anxiety, and absolute destitution I felt daily was inexplicable. I was a person who had even been to therapy and had no relief. I had read a ton of financial advice books, hired money coaches, and even gone through an expensive online school to get better with generating money. It wasn't until I read one book that spoke about recovery in relation to money that I was able to learn that my situation was not hopeless, that I was not alone, and that I could recover. I learned that although my childhood experiences, social conditions and current location all worked in favor of my disease, I could retrain my mind, my body, and my spirit to operate in ways that supported my recovery instead of my disease. I learned that indeed, working with others was a solution, that program did work, and that a renewed spiritual connection to my Higher Power could facilitate it all.

As women with various recovery experiences, we are writing with all of the questions, concerns and skepticism that shows up in recovery, and especially in regard to finances. There are so many people in pain around the world due to the compulsive behaviors around money that they simply cannot break through on their own. This book is for you, to show you that recovery is possible, that we can have a daily reprieve from our compulsive behaviors, and most importantly, that you are not alone. Please allow our stories to offer you experience, strength and hope that you too, with the help of program, the steps and your fellowship can experience recovery.

Chapter Two

Creating Your Own Recovery: Expect Great Changes!

Batya from Ohio

When I came back into Underearners Anonymous (UA) the second time, in October of 2015, I had literally thousands of dollars of unpaid hospital bills all over my bedroom floor, covering the tabletop in my office, and all over the dining room table. I could hardly walk around in my own house, and not only because I was recovering from three surgeries from a smashed ankle after a motorcycle had hit me while I was biking on Isla Mujeres, in Mexico. Even though before the accident, having been in the program since April of 2012, I thought I had things pretty much under control, I was also afraid of losing one of my jobs. I felt very run down from trying to get the claims met by the various insurance companies before the job I had ran out. I was bewildered about how I could get reimbursed for what I had put on credit cards to get my first two surgeries in a hospital in Mexico. I began clinging to the 7:15 a.m. solvency telephone call in the morning, every morning, to help me get out of bed. I felt so overwhelmed, powerless, and hopeless, on my own, fighting with hospitals and insurance companies, and panicked about the loss of my main adjunct online teaching job. I spoke once on one of these calls. I said I was calling from Cleveland. Somebody asked for my number. She called. She said she had worked as an astrology reader and wanted to give me a reading. I immediately became suspicious. The woman on the other side of the phone said she just had heard how much pain and confusion I was in and wanted to help. But I felt this was a trap, that she wanted to make some money off me. She wanted to charge; I was sure. But, she didn't. She actually worked as a claims adjuster in the health insurance business, though I did not find that out until much later. She offered to give me a reading only after I told her that I worked as a tarot reader. I don't even know how that came up.

About the bills-- she told me to do a little bit a day, to look at the process like sweeping the floor. That I might not finish or see progress in a day, but that I would be making a stab at the process. She quipped some Buddhist phrases: Before enlightenment, chop wood, haul water. After enlightenment, chop wood, haul water. Something penetrated. Trying to get the insurance companies to process and settle things, to do their part, was just a menial task that I had to perform every day. I asked her to be my sponsor, right away. Well, she said, why don't you try answering the step guide questions, and read me your answers, one at a time. You can call me once a day.

And so, I did. Every day I wrote an answer, and every day I called this magical person and read her an answer. By the answer to Question 19, she said yes, she would be my sponsor.

It wasn't until years later that I found out the only reason she had asked for my number was location. As they say in real estate, location, location, location. She used to live in Cleveland, which is where I had said on the line I was calling from. Also, years later, I found out that she had asked me to answer the step-guide questions first to see if I was serious, and ready to do the work. She was screening me, in a way. I don't know where all those answers I wrote out so intensely and furiously then are now, but I wrote as if my life depended upon the answers I wrote to share. I suppose my life actually did depend on this exchange, at the time.

[Wait. I just found a few, which I wrote and read to my sponsor]:

Question 14:

Discuss and reflect on how you have used the substitution method instead of accepting a higher power in your life. Are you still looking for substitutes? Explore. *I am not sure what the substitution method is or where I am supposed to read about it, but I suppose it means, substituting something else for higher power? I suppose I look to my family, friends; to the system of work; to the idea of reward for work done; to the courts and the system of justice.*

Also explore open mindedness--*open minded enough to say I need to develop my own system to keep track of time; to consider maybe my reaction was abnormal or that I could be reacting another way to the course cut backs; that my resistance to tracking might be the same resistance to charting the money originally, that I don't want to look at how much I am doing that doesn't earn anything because it will make me angry at myself and bring on the self-hate and self-blame*

Willingness—*to follow the suggestions of the sponsor; to be open to getting health care for free at the clinic instead of holding on to the insurance the university gives me; to find or regain the spiritual basis of life; to admit I had lost touch with god; and no longer had faith;*

Honesty—*to admit I wasn't successfully time charting yet; to admit there were problems in the survival system I had set up; to admit I felt doomed and that this feeling was propelling me down the rabbit hole faster; to admit, I had touched and been touched very strongly before by the vast spirit of human intelligence but honestly, I could not believe in any hp anymore; lost my ability to connect with happiness because I wasn't connecting with spirit any more through dance, painting; to admit that I have laid the groundwork pretty well for the place in Floyd and the place in Mexico...that I got the car and kept the van so things are going ok...that I am keeping the journal going too and publishers are asking me for books if I choose to follow through with them*

Question 15

Belief means reliance, not defiance. *I could not find this in the 12 and 12, but I guess it means, if you have belief in a higher power, you can have faith that there is a force greater than yourself managing to take care of things out there and helping you so you don't have to defy reality and fight against it tenaciously to try to build on to what you have gt at all costs, trying to alter or change the situation so desperately. You can believe that there is a higher order, that God has more in mind for you, a plan, and trust that you can be supported by the universe and just move on.*

Defiance is an outstanding characteristic of every under earner*. P.31 Defiance comes into play like when I lose a job, and I want to fight to keep it, or when the city wants to take me to court, or charge me for mowing the lawn when they have mowed down my mint crop, and when I pray for results the way I want them, instead of the best possible outcome...sometimes I pray for the ability to deal with things—is that defiance? I put in the intention of doing bills, housework—is that defiance, as in a way it is asking for help, for HP to grease and oil what I want, like a clean house, bills paid, and so on. Maybe I should just pray for the ability to do what HP wants me to do today...I have been having this impression growing of writing a Twelve and Twelve for Under-earners....I looked at the Hazelton and they want two who chapters...so I decided no, but writing two chapters might be a good experience for me anyway. I could at least read the twelve and twelve of AA and the 12 and 12 of OA and compare, take notes, and see what the differences are very carefully...*

The hoop you have to jump through is a lot wider than you think *p.26 I think this must refer to the belief in spirituality or a higher power doesn't have to be a narrow definition of God, the one we were conditioned to believe in during childhood. Our idea of Higher Power might be expanded to include any creative force we feel around us operating in the universe, or any evidence we can see in the universe, like the power that makes the grass grow, and seeds turn into trees reaching up to the sky...]*

This woman listened to all this gibberish every morning for most of October of 2015. In the process of becoming my sponsor, she told me to write down the phone numbers of everyone who offered their numbers on every call. And to keep a notebook of each person's name, where they were from, the date I first called, and whether they called back. If they didn't, move on. Why I had asked. Because you are building a support network she answered. You want reliable people, not flakes.

I honestly didn't even know what a reliable support network was. Or that I could build one. Or how to distinguish between reliable people and flakes. Or that I deserve reliable people to work with around me and supporting me. And that I could be reliable too. I learned all that in UA.

Eventually, those outstanding hospital bills got paid by the insurance companies, and they also reimbursed me for the thousands I had laid out. I indeed lost that job and moved on to other ones. I got my health insurance needs fulfilled in other ways. HP created other streams of income for me.

But I remember by the time I was in Step Three, something happened in one of the phone calls with someone in one of the insurance companies. I used the language of Step Three, about recognizing that only a force larger than myself was going to be able to solve this, when talking to him, to this voice on the other side. The person on the other side of the phone must have been in recovery himself because he started to open all these doors for me. He got the insurance company in MX to communicate with his insurance company. The eight thousand dollars I had unnecessarily paid to the hospital in Cancun upon admittance (because otherwise the operation would not have been performed) was reimbursed. He was able to clarify that the insurance company should have paid the hospital, and so therefore the insurance company had to pay me, and the situation was resolved. Everything changed. So, you often hear that phrase, in program? Wait for the miracle? This was most assuredly one of them for me. Now, every morning when I do my gratitude list, I realize I experience an HP-sponsored miracle every day of the week. On Monday at 9 AM, I have an hour-long *Red Book* study call with a partner from ACA, a program my second step sponsor in UA had recommended I try, so I did. On Tuesday, at 1 pm, I have an hour-long call with a work partner. Every other Wednesday, I have a regular call with someone who used to be a sponsee, and who is now a writing partner. Every Wednesday at 11:30 AM, I have an hour call with a UA partner with whom I am writing and editing this book. On Thursday, regularly, at 10, I have a self-care UA partner call; at 10 AM Friday, I have a regular UA Academic partner call; sometimes she and I schedule two- or three-hour parallel work sessions on various days of the week. On every other Saturday at 3:30 pm, I have a regular numbers partner call. Between 8 and 9 every evening, I have a regular tenth step partner call. And on Sunday every 8 pm, I have a regular three-way action meeting call.

Guess who has developed a regular support system? Me! This is what recovery looks like, for me. Am I recovered? Oh, I am not done. I still nosedive. I still have relapses. But when I do, I have someone on one of these spokes of my personally developed recovery wheel who will say, sounds like you need to do a step three on that, or a step four ...or someone who might say, I have heard you sound down before. Or, I might hear someone say, thanks so much. You really helped me a lot. Or you are doing a lot of work. You got so much done. Congrats on the self-care!

Or they are treating you terribly. What do you get out of that? Why go back? You are under-earning in that job! What is your vision! Walk away! Walk towards that! And when I remember to pray, and work the steps, I find that I actually can.

PART TWO

Benefits of Step Work

Chapter Three

Underearning and Family: Making Amends as a Parent

Ellen from NY

I have a 39-year-old son, but I've seen him only less than a dozen times since he was 12, which was about 6 years after his biological mother and I split up. He lives in the best and worst parts of my life – with joy and loss and pride and anger.

I'm a recovering debtor and underearner. I've worked the Debtors Anonymous program for over 30 years and have learned more about my issues from Underearners Anonymous. I highly recommend both. Unfortunately, my recovery began after my ex and I split up. That's also why it began – because I suddenly was paying the rent and utilities by myself. And it took years before my income allowed me to pay my bills on time and completely because my recovery included going back to school for over 5 years. By then, I was able to see my son only once a month because my ex had a five-year plan to remove me from his life. She succeeded by the following year.

That's when my underearning really impacted my relationship with him. For one thing, he was aware that I didn't have enough money to pay for his tennis lessons anymore, and as a pre-adolescent he took that to mean I had never done anything for him. I was also dependent on free legal advice, which dissuaded me from going to court. I didn't have the funds needed to set a precedent for same-sex parenting. I also didn't have the experience gained in DA to research options. But even prior to then, we had friends who set up a legal contract to ensure that the non-biological mother would continue to have access to their daughter if they separated. However, we lacked the funds to do that, and I went into our parenting on faith and promises alone.

Recently, working the Steps with a DA sponsor, I wrote and sent a letter to my son as part on my 9th Step. I wanted him to know how much I loved and cared for him when he was young, how I had tried to maintain our relationship, and that my love for him remains unconditional. I hoped it would bring him additional self-knowledge and understanding of why I've wanted to be in his life through all the years since. I told him about his childhood, including the introduction of his father into his life at age 4 and the care he and I gave him during the illness my ex suffered after we separated. I talked about how I tried to remain in his life by arguing with my ex at every turn as she took him away from me, by seeking legal counsel that was afraid a judge would take him away from all three of us, and by appealing for help to her family and his father. I acknowledged all the difficulties he experienced, including the death of his father when he was 17.

I haven't heard from him in the 10 months since I sent the letter with photographs from his childhood. I didn't expect a response but did hope for one. In any case, I offered him love in a letter of amends. Now it's in the hands of my Higher Power and his.

Chapter Four

Steps Towards Gratitude

James from San Francisco

It is a well-known fact that the 12 Step Program is explained in the book Alcoholics Anonymous. All of the subsequent programs based on the 12 Steps (and there are many) refer those seeking recovery to the AA 12 Steps. The literature of the many related programs gives information directed to the specific addictions on which they focus. But the 12 Step Program as found in the first 164 pages of the AA Big Book (Alcoholics Anonymous) is the source of all of the 12 Step programs.

I found DA (Debtors' Anonymous) after being a member of AA for around 10 years. I must have heard someone mention DA. I don't remember who, or when. I needed help and must have looked up the website and found a meeting not far from where I lived. I went to a meeting and listened to various people talk about their situations. I heard some of the tools they used: DA and AA Literature, Meetings, Sponsorship, Pressure Relief Groups and Pressure Relief Meetings. After we have gained some familiarity with the D.A. program, we organize Pressure Relief Groups consisting of ourselves and two other recovering debtors who have not incurred unsecured debt for at least 90 days and who usually have more experience in the program. The group meets in a series of Pressure Relief Meetings to review our financial situation. These meetings typically result in the formulation of a spending plan and an action plan.

Recovery from compulsive debting begins when we stop incurring new, unsecured debt, one day at a time. We attain a daily reprieve from compulsive debting by practicing the 12 Steps and by using the tools. Having worked the Steps in AA with a sponsor prepared me to be open to the tools and the suggestions given to me when I talked to someone (I'll refer to them as B.) in the program about my situation with credit card debt. My situation was seemingly hopeless. B arranged for me to meet with his sponsee who a professional financial counselor was. I'll refer to the counselor as E. He seemed glad to meet with me.

I'd seen him in the rooms, but I hadn't met him. B. introduced us at a meeting and after the meeting E. and I got together for coffee at a cafe. He told me to request my credit scores from three companies. We'd meet again after I received the credit reports. He asked me how much I owed, how much the minimum payments were, how much was my income. I've been disabled and on a fixed income for some time. My debting had gone beyond my income. The minimum payments were more than half my income and I couldn't stop using the card. Each month the minimum was more and more. My income was eaten up by credit card debt I couldn't control. Only a few people knew how demoralized I was. It was strange to reach a bottom – the point at which my life seemed out of control. I wasn't homeless, I was clean and sober and yet I was a wreck around finances. Asking for help is something I might not have been able to do if I hadn't been in the rooms of AA.

The credit reports came, and I met with E. again. He looked at all three. I really didn'tunderstand them at that point. He explained. "I have good news, and ...mostly good news. You aren't planning to buy a house or a car anytime soon, are you?" No, far from it. My rent was subsidized and was on autopay, I had a cable bill and a phone bill. The credit card bill was my biggest bill.

"Well, basically, I'm going to give you some advice that I couldn't give you if you were an actual client of the company I work for. It's like this. You've never missed a payment to the bank, never been late, and as long as you don't plan to take out a loan for a house or a car you don't have to pay them. They trapped you. You're borrowing money from them to pay them. It's crazy. What you should do is close that account and open an account at a credit union."

He suggested one. "Put the money you've usually would pay to the bank into a savings account. The credit union doesn't charge for atm use, no penalty for overdraft. The bank will keep coming after you for a while, quite a while. Probably 7 years, but legally there's nothing they can do. They'd block you if you were applying for credit for a house or a car. They'll sell your debt to a collection agency, and you'll get calls. You'll have to put up with it. If it gets to be too much, you can apply for a cease-and-desist order."

This was like the second step. (Editors' note: Step 2: *Came to believe that a Power greater than ourselves could restore us to sanity.*) At that point I began to believe that there was a solution to my problem. And I followed his instructions. Kind of like a third step. (Editors' note: Step 3: M*ade a decision to turn our will and our lives over to the care of God as we understood Him.*) I got a debit card. I can only spend money I actually have. That's like the beginning of recovery in DA. No new debts. Not one. One day at a time. That was over ten years ago, and I haven't taken on any new debt.

There's more to my story, but that's for another time.

PART THREE

How We Work

Chapter Five

Progress Made: Seeing the City Where I Live as Beautiful

Chery from Orlando

Before UA, I used to feel I needed to get out of this town, I can't ever make it here, maybe I need to live in California where I was born, *etc. etc*. Though I had been involved in many programs of abundance, prosperity and positive self-talk, nothing really stayed with me until I was willing to take more responsibility for my choices. Coming out of hiding was a big lesson that was a major UA theme. Wanting to stay small, let someone else take care of me and never ever stand up for myself have emerged as major life lessons over the last ten years of my UA life. I have been in my own small business since 1998, working as a Healing Arts Specialist, Teaching Artist and Therapeutic Musician. Because many prospective employers to whom I market myself haven't heard of these occupations before or haven't even been aware of the value of this type of work, or aware that these are professions requiring training, skill, empathy and talent, many equate what I do with a voluntary offer. I educate them during my sales approach while presenting them with my prices. Nonetheless, as a deprivation addict, I felt that it was "normal" for companies I did independent contract work for to end up not paying me, dis my efforts, bully me or somehow put me down.

The only entity that was solid in payment to me was a Regional Medical Center, where I pioneered my programs for The Mind, Body, Medicine Center in the Cancer Institute working with at-risk youth in a psychiatric hospital. In the nursing home facilities, many events occurred involving women directors with a lot of bullying energy as well as some critical men. Because of my abusive history with these types of people, I used to want to run instead of stopping and speaking my truth or asking for what I needed.

For the last 10 years of being in UA, working the steps with a sponsor, having action and goals pages partners, giving service in meetings, and practicing how I would make stands for myself all paid off in my ability to stand up and speak to "scary" authority figures.
In one case, an affiliate of a local hospital where I facilitated bedside therapeutic music didn't communicate to me concerning the needed paperwork, I had to fill out so I could get paid in a timely manner. Finally, after a year of standing up, where I found myself capable of facing fear zones, they paid me everything due as of March 2020.

Working on my negative self-talk, listening to other UA members, counseling, and working with the Inner Child from the ACA program have each made a huge difference in the way I go forward to do the work and helped me stand up to be fairly compensated. I had to change an inner belief that I deserve to be used and abused as a Musical Caregiver. I am getting unstuck from a lifetime of living in a dysfunctional past.

In the last 5 years I have been able to show up in front of the activity directors, administrators and high-level management and ask for a fair price for this area of work that I do and for the value that I bring to their institutions. I learned how to announce my new pricing, when it will start and how much benefit the clients will receive. In some instances of a company going bankrupt after hiring me, I would be taken for another round of delayed payments and having to write the loss off my income tax as a bad debt. Many of the directors had a negative attitude when I followed up with my invoices. The last time this happened, I spoke to the administrator and activity director. Since they were both men, I felt intimidated and wanted to delay the process. I decided in addition to my calls, I would show up and make my case clear. I told them of my intention to stop my services until I received compensation and I followed through. I went to investigate small claims court, something I thought I would never do. It ended up that I didn't have to file a claim, but I was willing to do so which gave me a sense of power and a feeling of strength when I went back and negotiated. Finally, I found out that all of my standing up, calling and making appointments with CEOs and other administrators and withdrawal of my services helped to get me fully paid!

For the last year, I have been revamping my vision and goals, so I only take work for which I am promptly paid. For the last year, prior to the Covid 19 shutdown, I was working with temporary substitute teaching work through an agency, and I call this my G job. (G-d for short) since I was taking my music, teaching and therapeutic music skills into schools with daily work that paid weekly. Some days I was working with orchestral students, guitar ensembles and jazz bands! I loved the students' energy and creativity! I got to study my music theory, play music with them and get credit for therapeutic music C.E.U.'s.

This year I will meet my goal to complete all of my continuing education units for my profession. Instead of worrying and wondering who would pay, I was getting to the school assignments early and staying late. This is new behavior for me. I have learned in this program the value and necessity of structure with my time, diligence, and massive positive action.

Thank You UA, there are acres of diamonds in my backyard. I don't need to move to California to find my gold!

Chapter Six

Higher Power as I Understand it, or Notes from the Beach

Beatriz in Mexico

When I first had gotten back to Mexico on this island to which I have been coming to, on and off for over thirty years, so much had changed that I felt out of control. Oh yes. I had to surrender to Mexico. I was most definitely out of control. I just had to surrender to the chaos, to all the things I could not control. I could not control the noise, or the development, or the sudden spurts and growth of tourism, or the traffic. So yesterday I let the prayer beads tell me where to go and it was to Sabine's, where I saw the sunset --which was wonderful until the bugs came. I couldn't control those either. Then driving into town, I prayed to the goddess for a parking space and got that perfect one right where you turn left up by the church side where the sea wall is. I walked past Adrian's xerox and print shop and saw the sign for the one bedroom which was back up again. He was there and got his son to take me to see the room, which is right over the laundry so I can take my laundry in easier, and it has AC and hot water. The apartment is upstairs from Adrian's also, so I can get things printed more easily. It's almost as if god answered my prayers and brought me the perfect place. This morning I was thinking how I could get a bike if I live over there and can bike in the sunrise on the sea wall and get more exercise. It would be more like the old island when I used to have fun, biking down to market. It would even be easier to leave my dog in there on the bed and go into the supermarket when I need stuff.

So as soon as I let go and let god, the perfect place comes along. Of course, there are disadvantages so if he says no, it is ok, as Adrian didn't think the landlord would take a dog. Praying really helped restore me to sanity. Thank you, higher force.

It is, by the way, an interconnected force. Also happened with the *queso* salesperson walking with his megaphone and shoes. "*Tienes zapatos* now," I said. He used to walk barefoot belting his heart out. Now he carries a recording of himself yelling, "*queso, queso* Oaxaca" on a boom box machine. He asked me how I had been, and I said I had had work in the US, so I had been away for eleven months. This was my last time because the island had changed so much. Cancun had invaded the island. I told him about the place on the beach where the boat comes for Cancun Explorers. They have couch chairs and it's all roped off. The people sit there and there is a store for them and a restaurant. Everything is brought to them like the company Cancun Explorers has bought the beach. Yes, it's our president, he said. He sold us out. *Bajaste* he said, meaning I had lost weight. "And where will you go?" "India, Israel. Wherever I get work," I answered. He packed up my *cuarenta* pesos worth of Oaxaca cheese, made my change and went on.

I ate my *queso* with my cucumber. I cleaned the space, finding more notebooks I could read and ship away. I found the glue nails, and this helped me work on the walls without cement dust so I did that for a while including putting a nose and some mouth that had fallen off on a goddess on the street. Michelle came by and asked, "Beatriz, how are you. This is our last day. I was looking for you, to find out what happened with that terrible job you had?" I invited her in. We talked about how higher education was being increasingly controlled from the top down so people were retiring early where she was from. The union was saying they had to fight it, that adjunct pay was being cut and adjuncts were being cut; there was less and less academic freedom. We talked about how this was bad for the students and for civic society. She bought an IxChel Press publication that has the story of the goddess art project here too. I gave her the art installation card that has the map and let her know she could find us on google maps too.

Do you think this was a "god" day, since all these nice things happened once I got to Step Three and I let the power of god direct my life? I accepted help and this was what I got, good things blowing towards me all day and me being able to take small steps too. The spiritual guidance is just to go with the flow makes things much easier like unsticking everything although packing notebooks and things to send off is not going to be easy. It means going to Cancun. But I need to clear stuff out whether I stay or go. Today I threw out a Wi-Fi bill and a map of Brazil. I couldn't find where I had been in a community on it. So, it's just clutter. I found a Kate Millett picture from her memorial with a couple of quotes and used one this morning and put the sheet inside. I found paints so I didn't need to buy any more.... oh well.

Now I seek guidance from this interconnected flow of the universe every time I get stuck or ambivalent. So... Should I call on the apartment or not? I'm going to use the mala bead bracelet I got at Amma's.... call don't call from beginning to end. OK it says don't call for now. How about going down to see Letty this afternoon. Yes, this says go so I better rest up and walk down....

So, by the time I rested up I lit the candles here and did the beads again and got to stay in. More writing on this....there is no guide to connecting with the interconnective force for most of us....the Chasidic Jews have the rules down to the very last detail and for a while it was fun to share when I was going for Chanukah but seeing the seclusion of the women on Shabbat I just don't feel I can partake or that I belong there, and as to why I did not go see Letty-- my knee hurt so I just stayed in and emptied the drawer of papers where I had sprayed for the roach before...I bleached it and found the packet I had started for Duke archives before. So now I have one notebook to add to it. I am getting a lot from reading notebooks, like how it is always noisy when I try to sleep here and how it is always hard to get stuff done....the silly fights with Beto the vendor down the street over the screen door….now I have turned to him about somebody he might find to fix my roof but why…I wanted to ask the Colombian because he sent me a great electrician and it was Bonnie who sent me the great carpenter who actually built such good solid things, which shows the benefit of going with the interconnected flow….not just taking from whomever is around you and leaning on them. Anyway, my knee is not in a flow. I took a tramadol. And so, I managed to throw some papers out from the drawer as well as the last cockroach, I hope.

Even perfect belief in a perfect god would probably not make me happy. I like having to recreate what I have faith in all the time although it takes up more time. This means I go through more repeated spiritual crises than some of those people in the tight spiritual fundamentalist groups who have their clear god and their clear rules. I am always making mine up to turn to. Today and yesterday, I felt my soul in my body as I tossed in the waves to the shore. That is where I find that interconnected force. Right there. When I am completely relaxed, I feel the force within. No, it's kind of a mesh like a web within me that is woven of this white brilliant emanating material. This is god or the interconnecting force. Yet force is a hard word. What I really mean is the divinity that interconnects and weaves us all together as one. I enjoy floating and being brought gently to the shore right in that place. Right in that part where the sea meets the beach, where the sparkles come from, where the sparkles are within and without. That is the god force, that is the higher power or infinite intelligence. Or maybe flow is the term a sponsor once used and what I am looking for. The connecting lattice is what I would say now, perhaps. Bit by bit, I feel this connectedness of the inner and outer from the inside, which now I have learned that Buddhists such as Thich Nhat Hanh would refer to as the interbeing. So, every day I go there to the place where the sea meets the sand when I can and relax and float. Until this morning, although I was enjoying being the only one in the water on the entire expanse of the beach. I couldn't believe I really was alone, that there were no tourists taking selfies. No twenty-year-olds with their butts hanging out over the straps of their bikinis, no boys playing with sword toys, no one smoking cigarettes on the beach. Just me. I was in such absolute bliss until I smelled a whiff of gasoline waft past my nose from a boat and had to get out, fast. I walked home just in time to get a phone call made. Back to the to do list. Back to my compulsions. Almost forgetting god.

Bit by bit though, this is my god I get every day, when I go to the sea. I go every morning that I can. It's my spiritual practice, which allows me to carry the web within. Thus giving me peace, a feeling of connection to everyone, to my true rather than false self and most importantly to divinity throughout the day.

Chapter Seven

Surviving the Quarantine with Honesty, Openness and Willingness: A Twelve Step Concept

Mel from New York

It has to work.

It has to work.

It has to be different this time.

This is my last chance.

This is it.

I can't wind up homeless.

This has to work.

It has to be different this time.

"Yeah, but how…???"

And that's when I paused in my panic.

Literally clutching my head trying to steel myself into figuring out how to rescue my life from an overnight shutdown of my business, I stopped…no, actually, I was stopped. A voice said, "Honesty. Openness. Willingness. That's how." (We find that no one need have difficulty with the spirituality of the program. *Willingness, honesty and hope mindedness are the essentials of recovery. But these are indispensable*-- AABB *567 Appendix II)* And in that moment, the dawning of clarity began to emerge in my being. My soul opened up, and I felt the spirit of the universe move into me. It was as if I surrendered, in Step Three. (Step Three *Made a decision to turn our will and our lives over to the care of God as we understood God.*)

We were in quarantine. All of us. The entire planet. We were sequestering inside. People were dying in droves. Big business had taken the first round of fiscal aid. And we were all holding our breath.

There was a palpable quiet in the air. I could feel our collective fear, all of it, in all of us. We were afraid to leave the house, afraid to look at one another, afraid to touch anything. We were all afraid and uncertain. Something was in the air that could kill us, and there was nothing we could do to stop it.

My business, a small natural medicine practice that I had grown solvently for the last nine years, was shut down overnight. I'd carefully managed my money and my numbers to make sure I could divorce my husband without harming myself financially, something I had a history of doing countless times in my life. I had just started recovering from the paranoia that told me he was having me followed, just like my father had done to my mother. I was just beginning to sleep easily at night, having begun to recover from the fear that he would break in and rape me in the middle of the night, just like my father had done to my mother. I was still sleeping with the closet doors open – because my father jumped out of the closet with a knife in his teeth and raped my mother one night when she came home from work. This happened while I was sleeping in the other room.

I was just climbing out from under this blanket of terror, just recovering from the sudden death of my younger brother, killed in a hit-and-run overseas, right at the height of his happiness and newly created freedom.

I felt betrayed and abandoned by Life itself. I did all the things I was supposed to do. I followed the instructions. I surrendered, as in Step Two (Editors' Note: *Came to believe that a Power greater than ourselves could restore us to sanity.*). I was a good girl. I did what I was told. I kept my numbers, a tool of DA (Editors' Note DA Tool 2. Record Maintenance: *We maintain records of our daily income and expenses, of our savings, and of the retirement of any portions of our outstanding debts.*). I paid my bills on time and over-paid my taxes.

And there I was…walking my apartment in a panic…clutching my head…trying to figure out how to generate income that would keep me from winding up homeless, just like my mother said I would.

Thankfully, I'd joined DA a few weeks before quarantine. I was afraid of myself, of what I do with money. I knew that my fear of myself vis a vis money was one of the things preventing me from filing for divorce. I was afraid. Of myself and all the unconscious messages that drove me to money drunkenness. As a woman I heard in an OA (Overeaters Anonymous) meeting once said: *I'm afraid of being by myself because it puts me alone in the room with the only person who has ever tried to kill me.*

Well, I've come to discover that I might not be the only one who's ever tried to kill me (that's a story for another day). But there I was then. Quarantine. Deadly virus. No income. Worst fears possibly coming true. And me. Always me.

And honesty.
And openness.
And willingness.

There was the answer. Once I felt the peace and clarity of hearing the message come through, I started to believe again; STEP THREE. I started to believe that doing the work would actually yield the results AND STOP THE COMPULSION. I'd stopped believing that decades ago. I just never realized it until I got into recovery. So, I started to believe again. I remembered that I could trust recovery. I could trust God. Faith. That no matter what happened, I would continue to embrace it all as the manifestation of God's will for my life.

There's so much more to this story to tell. Receiving the message that night – Honesty. Openness. Willingness. – sobered me up to hear the voice of universal consciousness answering my plea. It was real. It is real. It is here. Always. And all I have to do is live three simple principles.

That's HOW.

Chapter Eight

A Higher Power of My Own Understanding

Lynda from Virginia

Having been brought up in a very strict religious Christian upbringing in which my siblings and I were sent to boarding school at six years of age so that my parents could do the Lord's work as missionaries, I carried a lot of rage around me about God, who was not a loving force in my estimation. The phrase. God's Will has been an anathema to me. In my experience, God's Will was not benign. God's Will meant doing that which we did not want to do. It meant my parents sacrificing their children in the name of God. My concept of God was a very negative one. Nature and beauty were my solace.

It wasn't until I started doing the 12 steps that I was given permission to develop a higher power of my own understanding. (Editors' Note: Step 3 *Made a decision to turn our will and our lives over to the care of God as we understood God.*) Years ago, in a third-step workshop, a sponsor asked me to name a higher power that I could live with. Two words came to me. They were Exuberant Fecundity. I had never used these two words in my vocabulary, so I looked them up in the dictionary. Exuberant represents joy, and fecundity characterizes fertility and productivity. These words animate my actions as an artist.

Over the years, I experienced family loss and tragedy. My step-daughter had a traumatic brain injury in a motorcycle accident, leaving my husband and I to raise her three children. My husband died of cancer, and tragically, my grandson who we raised committed suicide. The 12 steps, meetings, literature and telephone calls have kept me grounded in gratitude for the gifts that I have been given in spite of these tragedies. The phrase, Exuberant Fecundity, offers a navigational point for where I should turn when I am stuck in indecision.

The art I do is a source of healing for myself and hopefully for others. I am reminded of the Iraqi cellist, Karim Wasfi, who played his instrument at the time of bloodshed and havoc in Baghdad in defiance of violence. It was a gesture to overcome insanity by acts of beauty and creativity.

As a creator who has often questioned my work as an artist, Exuberant Fecundity has allowed me to continue to create, and to even find success, community and prosperity as a creative.

PART FOUR

Working With Tools

Chapter Nine

90-in-90 UA Style

Lisa in Northern California

Though I was not new to 12-step recovery programs, it only took a few UA phone meetings for me to recognize that this was the program in which I wanted to do my first ever 90 in 90, which in recovery circles means going to ninety meetings in ninety days. In a sense, making that commitment was my very first step away from chronic underearning: though I'd always enjoyed my program meetings, felt good when I was in a meeting, and valued the recovery I found through the steps, traditions, tools and fellowship, I had never allowed myself the gift of receiving that goodness every day.

I had been practicing scarcity and deprivation, underearning and underbeing in the sense that what could make me feel good was readily, freely, and abundantly available to me on a daily basis, but I did not believe I could have it every single day—I had heard of others doing 90 meetings in 90 days. (Editors' Note: UA Tool 2 *Meetings – We attend UA meetings regularly to share our experience, strength, and hope in order to help ourselves and others recover from underearning.*) Every single one of them reported that the process was an amazing lift to their recovery and so worth it, yet I still didn't believe that could be for me. "Wow, that sounds so inspiring and helpful!" I'd think, while simultaneously suspending belief that it was something *I* could do.

I had a list of ready excuses, the number one excuse being of course I didn't have time. What I'd not yet been ready to admit was that I was capable of allowing time, *creating* the time in my life to make the commitment. That attitude, that persistent and helpless belief of not having enough time pervaded every aspect of my life and sapped the energy out of everything I loved to do—every single thing.

It wasn't until I was desperate: I'd returned to grad school to finish my MA and had a mental breakdown during my postpartum period with an unexpected third child. Discovering that I needed a divorce and had no way, no clue of how to go about supporting myself, I felt deeply defective—like a jellyfish washed up on the beach. I couldn't scoot, crawl, or even belly flop my way back to the water.

I realized I'd never been self-supporting at any time in my life. I had no idea of how to nurture my skills and talents and whole self, no way to even get in touch with what my needs really were. Though I began that process of self-discovery and self-love on my own and with the support of other 12-step programs, it was another two years before the tide swelled, picked me up from the beach, and I found my way into UA.

When I began hearing terms like "underbeing," "hiding and biting," "time drunk," "exertion and exhaustion," and "museum states," I knew I'd finally homed in on the core of my chronic ineffectivity and unhappiness. I attended a couple of phone meetings and then committed myself to a 90 in 90. I have three children and had been through three pregnancies which lasted 24 hours a day for 9 months—surely one hour a day for 90 days was easy compared to that!

I think the biggest effect of the 90 in 90 was that the experience broke the inertia of the fear-based paralysis that held me in stasis for so long. Consistent meetings became an opportunity to practice a new way of being in small increments of time. I already knew I liked meetings. I liked how they made me feel. I attended meetings where the focus was on allowing ourselves to receive not only more financial abundance, but more *actual abundance* arising from recognizing that goodness and good feelings are abundant in the world. I learned that reaching for that goodness and abundance is literally as easy as dialing a telephone number and taking one hour of the day to suspend my disbelief in the possibility of abundance for me. I could listen to what others had to say about it. I didn't even need to "suit up" to show up! I could be in my pajamas, I could be in the bathtub, I could be on a walk.

My 90 in 90 really helped me begin the process of allowing myself to align with my higher power's will for me before I even started picking up the tools or working the steps: showing up every day was a sort of affirmation that yes, my Higher Power really did want me to experience happiness every single day of my life, and I only had to show up one day at a time. At first, I didn't even have to believe all day every day that I could be happy—I could count on a meeting to give me some little inspirations that perked me up, and then no matter what feelings or resistance arose during the rest of the day, I knew I'd be getting help again tomorrow. Attending daily meetings was a lot more like having "God on call" than I'd ever experienced in my previous seven years of program work. Daily fellowship was exciting for the parts of me that enjoy exertion, that enjoy freshness and newness and possibility to make a 90-day commitment, yet safe for the parts of me that warily get dragged behind those parts! I could do just 90 days, and I could do it one day at a time.

Going to a meeting everyday really helped me build momentum practically effortlessly. I didn't have to "work" at it—all I had to do was remember I wanted recovery and then dial up a meeting. I was getting such a rich daily influx of experience, strength, and hope, that my confidence was boosted in picking up new tools I'd never used before. I didn't feel compelled to use the tools, I didn't feel afraid of what would happen if I didn't use the tools—I was simply inspired and empowered to begin using them bit by bit as I was ready. I was encouraged by others to be gentle with myself, gentle with my learning process and gentle with the reality that growth takes time— all I really ever had was time!

A 90 in 90 set a pace for me that made it easier to slow down to being present in more moments. It was like my whole life got the opportunity to reorient itself gently and efficiently, as my growth in the program unfolded smoothly day by day, with this new way of being at the center, the core. I also got to sample so many different meetings in a short time that I quickly found the grooves that served me best. Nothing about my recovery felt rushed or urgent. Progress felt easy.

Another fun aspect of the 90 in 90 was that each 30 days brought its own set of shifts, but the structure of a meeting a day kept me supported through each one—especially as the initial momentum had worn off and I felt like I was losing steam. I'd forget meetings I'd penciled into my calendar for earlier in the day, and then look up new ones I hadn't tried yet.

For a couple of weeks near the end, I would forget every day but there was a meeting at 9:15pm in my time zone that I could catch! Once or twice, I was 15 minutes late to even that one! Once I had to attend the second half of an international meeting that was an hour before midnight my time, and then practice that gentleness with myself that I knew my Higher Power was feeling.

Through this process I learned my Higher Power was better at ordering my time than I was: sometimes I made a plan to attend a meeting at 10:30 am, but forgot, so then I'd plan for one at 4, and something would come up and I'd miss that one. The 90 in 90 commitment made it possible for me to not simply give up after having "failed." I knew to relax (if I had to settle for a 91 in 90, that would be okay) and trust myself. I practiced doing the next right thing: check the website for the next possible meeting that day.

So often whenever that happened, I'd end up hearing exactly what I needed to hear at the meeting I was at "by mistake" because I'd "messed up" remembering earlier meetings. Over and over I allowed myself to be delighted by the way my very simple decision to commit to a 90 in 90 gave my Higher Power the room in my life to show me not only how perfect every seeming "delay" or "mistake" on my part really was, but how cleverly it could play with me and delight me, because I was finally willing to be practice being happy every day for at least one hour longer than I'd ever let myself before. I didn't have to worry about keeping it up for life, I only had to keep it up for three months—and I only had to do that one day at a time.

The best effects of the 90 in 90 have been lasting so far. I started many daily practices, little by little, growing my life bigger and happier and more full of what I love as I went. The expansion was like opening up one tiny door after another, bit by bit as I was ready for a little more. I had the steady consistent stream of daily program wisdom and fellowship every day to help me do it. I run every day now, make time to stretch and move my body with yoga or dance. I let myself skip and hop and be playful as I go about different tasks. I daydream, I meditate daily, I make time to let myself feel the future I want to create for myself every day. I let myself listen to music that makes me happy more often. I take action steps readily when my Higher Power reveals them to me: I no longer feel compelled to force myself to take actions that aren't in my best interest. I no longer fear failure or mistakes. I understand we learn by doing, because I practiced it steadily for 90 days in a row. I work toward my creative visions in small chunks on a weekly basis. I take steps toward my career in small portions. I do housework with more joy; I organize with better discernment and humor and patience than before. I practice possession consciousness. (Editors' Note: UA Tool 4 *Possession Consciousness – We routinely discard what no longer serves us in order to foster a belief that life is plentiful and that we will be able to provide ourselves with what we need.*)

I follow my impulses more often, because I can trust them more now: practicing more happiness has made behaviors and habits that lead to unhappiness less tolerable to me, which has helped them shed or drop away completely, gradually and gently. I can follow the little ideas that flow into my mind, like, take this route instead of this one—and then let my Higher Power line me up with fun, sweet, inspiring, peaceful and beautiful little miracles incrementally on a daily basis. I learned that I'm worth taking good care of, and I learned it by starting to consistently practice self-care, with the daily help of the program. My life, my time, feels bigger than ever before, so full. Museum states[1] are less appealing and more recognizable than they were. I know now to rest through them, not criticize, compare, or despair.

---

[1] Museum States are defined by one of UA's founders as a pattern of repeating past behaviors or positions such as living on the edge, accepting less, being in constant struggle and constant comparison.
These were discussed at the UA Blasting out of the Cave event in San Francisco in June of 2017.
https://www.youtube.com/watch?v=oMHRq3VmzEA&list=PLWLEHh-Q3Wt7rgyaKsBK47ehJXDmm4fzh&index=10

My 90 in 90 was like a nice consistent cocoon in which I got to live my life, letting old habits gel and reform themselves. Shortly after my 90 in 90, I made a sudden realization that YES, I was ready to live happily ever after. I was ready to commit to being happy every single day for the rest of my life. I knew this didn't mean I would never again feel negative emotions or face difficulties and challenges, but I had been so deeply transformed by the experience of even that short term commitment, that I realized my own being had committed itself fully to my life long before my 90 in 90 helped my brain finally shed the baggage it was holding so it could start catching up.

Chapter Ten

Willingness: A Twelve Step Concept

Felicia from Vermont

My first 12-step program was not one expressly about finances. When I joined that program, I certainly was not using the UA tool of solvency (Editors' Note: UA Tool 9 Solvency: *We do not debt one day at a time. Debiting leads to underearning*): I had enough debt so that my credit card was returned more than once. A wealthy friend had made me a large loan, and I used the money to pay my bills. I was stuck in graduate school, unable, or so it seemed, to finish the work that would allow me to complete my degree and land a permanent job. I had just been a finalist for two excellent jobs in my field and lost them both to other candidates, partly, no doubt, because I hadn't graduated.

My career failures were not my only challenges in those days. Just as much as my other self-defeating behavior, the mess I was making of my career formed a sharp end of a menacing spear, one of the big sources of pain that brought me to the 12-step program. I was blessed then with the gift of desperation, which made me teachable. I went to hours of meetings, made mountains of phone calls (including to people I was pretty sure detested me, or had no idea who I was), got a sponsor I didn't know how to use, journaled like mad, listened more closely than I'd ever listened before. Then I heard about the 7th Tradition, our precious principle of self-support (Editors' Note: 7. *Every UA group ought to be fully self-supporting, declining outside contributions.*). I started contributing to the meetings I attended, sometimes with only a quarter in the basket, but always with something.

I came to believe that the cavalry wasn't coming to bail me out. My brilliance wasn't going to get me a job for which I wasn't fully qualified – or get me through an interview my insecurities were determined to screw up. So, with the help of the tools and steps of the program, I gained the ability to look at my part in my situation and started getting my act together with my career and behaving responsibly with my finances. I got up at 5 a.m. to write my thesis every day for about six months, and then the work for my degree was nearly done. I asked friends in the program for tips on how to do an effective job interview. After several more tries, a renowned university offered me a permanent job. I learned to pay people back when they made me a temporary loan, even if *I knew for a fact* that they didn't need the funds. When I received a windfall, I gave all of the money to the rich friend who helped me in graduate school. I took it on faith that since I was doing the right thing, the money I needed would arrive through other means.

Who knows what might have happened if I had kept working my original program as hard as I worked it in the first year? Instead of doing that, I eased up and had more challenges. I alienated many of the people I worked with. I didn't build social or professional networks. Thanks to fear and perfectionism, I spent longer writing my first book than I needed to. I wound up being scooped by a colleague who wrote on nearly the same subject. I lost my job, in part because of the delay with the book, and in part because I had isolated myself instead of building connections with the people I worked with. They didn't know me, hadn't had the chance to share their feedback on my work while it was in process, and were not deeply invested in my success. Since positions in my field are few and far between, this meant that, at the end of my contract, my partner and I had to sell our home and move. I considered leaving my field entirely and returning to the career I had before my graduate training. My partner and I spent most of our savings readying the house for sale (deferred maintenance seems entirely consistent with the symptoms of UA. [Editors' Note: UA Symptom 4. *Clinging to Useless Possessions – We hold onto possessions that no longer serve our needs, such as threadbare clothing or broken appliances.*]) and supporting ourselves as we worked part-time while looking for work and getting ready to move.

I was both lucky and willing. I suited up and showed up in what were then my two 12-step Programs (Al-Anon and Overeaters Anonymous). I learned a little about humility. At the end of a long search, with sometimes-faltering faith that things would turn out well, I secured an excellent job in my field. My spouse and I found a home we could afford, in a condo community that denied us the option to defer maintenance. She re-created her career and found something she truly loves and in which she is a great success. I learned to get along better with people at work, to follow directions, to be kinder to those around me. By the time I was evaluated for promotion, I was nearly a shoo-in. I received unanimous votes at every stage of the process.

So why UA? Well, my promotion and happy life in my new home community weren't the end of the story. I suffered – oh! The self-created drama!! – over choosing the subject of my second book. I spun wheels and wasted time creating and then backing away from multiple topics. I had an idea for a relatively simple project, but then let my perfectionism run the show and conceptualized a book that was so ambitious and complex that it terrified me. Ultimately, I dropped the idea because I feared the ambitious project would take a decade or more to write.

In the middle of this wheel-spinning, I started obsessing about the financial status and decisions of a couple of family members. I knew enough about 12-step recovery to realize that if other people's behaviors were bothering me so much – if I was deep in fear about them "dragging me down" – then I had a problem myself. Friends in Debtors Anonymous directed me to local DA meetings. I admired the rigor of that program, but debt wasn't my issue, so I didn't stay. However, my DA buddies were creating a local meeting of a program that I had never heard of before, Underearners Anonymous. *That* was a great fit: I knew that I was earning ok but not enough so that I could comfortably help my financially suffering family members, whom I genuinely wanted to help.

I had no idea how to increase my income, or to shift my ideas about my income.

On the strength of a very imperfect UA program, I made a start. First, while learning the program's language and concepts, I shared honestly about my situation. I pointed myself toward earning more, myself, so that I would not feel so anxious every time my partner and I considered following through on a generous impulse. I calmed down enough to choose a topic and a collaborator for my second book. The book was not any more perfect than my infant program: it's clear to me now that I failed to do what the Beyond Six Figures meetings of UA call "the proper business analysis." I wrote with a very qualified colleague who was also difficult for me to work with. I did a poor job of communicating my intentions, so she was surprised when I said I wanted to reach a fairly wide audience, not just experts in our field – and she refused to do it my way. Still, we finished and published the book. It did not make me a multi-millionaire or a household name. But it helped me reach some of my goals. The most important of these was another promotion at work, which came with an increase in my base salary, the retirement contributions based on that salary, and a gratifyingly fancy title.

While I was finishing that second book, my mother had a stroke during a family celebration and died. Seven months later, my father received a terminal diagnosis. Six months after that, he too died. In my grief and confusion, I backed away from program and slowed down the pace of my professional work. Thankfully, though, I never left UA or my other programs entirely. Thankfully, it did not occur to me to drop my spiritual or religious life. A couple of months after Dad died, I started, for the first time in my life, to pray at weekly services in the religion in which I was raised. I continued seeking and getting solace and guidance in the 12 Steps.

The most consistent, life-changing part of my UA program has been my Goals Group[2]. Originally this was a group of five, now four,

---

[2] Goals Group: a combination of UA Tools 6 and 8: *6. Goals Pages – We set goals for all aspects of our lives, write them down, measure our progress and reward achievement.*
8. Action Partner – We connect regularly with action partners regarding earning concerns in order to provide each other with accountability, continuity, and

professional writers. We all have years of experience in 12-step recovery and are committed to UA. We have been meeting once a week, with occasional breaks when life happens, for over four years. During that time, three of us, all published writers who had spent more time than necessary completing a manuscript, completed our books. One had a best-seller. Another received a glowing review in the *New York Times*. I received my promotion and boost in salary and status. I also applied for and won a year-long research position at one of the leading universities in the world – where, thanks to Higher Power, my program network and skillful negotiating, I made a good deal more money than at my home institution.

The most important aspect of our Goals Group is the way in which we hold each other accountable. Thanks to the UA Goals Pages, from which we read and write on one question per week, each of us has had a chance to outline and then refine our visions for our lives and careers. Under the umbrella of that large vision, we have specified what we want to do and create in the medium-term future. When we give feedback to one another, we don't get too involved in the specifics of what each person promises from week to week; we all have program buddies, sponsors, action partners, plus a subconscious mind, to remind us when we fail to do something. Instead, we hold each other accountable for living in accordance with our visions, both the big overarching vision and the specific projects that we have identified as roads to those visions.

The work I have done in the Goals Group allowed me to declare that I want to be a public intellectual. In fact, the group helped me realize that I am one, and that my new goal is to become a financially successful one with a bigger audience. With this in mind, I used some of the money I inherited from my mother to hire a publicist, who helped me share the message of my second book. I then found the subject of my third book, which I have designed from the start to reach audiences beyond experts in my field. On the strength of a small amount of writing and a lot of passion, I found a prominent literary agent who was willing to work with me. As I write this, I am waiting to hear the agent's feedback on the third draft of my book outline. Thank heaven that I am still teachable.

---

support. For more information on this, see the Resources document entitled "How to Run a Writers Goals Group" at the end of this book.

So far this year, I have done a major research presentation at the university where I was in residence, published two articles in a political opinion journal, appeared on local television, testified before a legislative committee, and published an op-ed in a newspaper that reaches influential people statewide. Tomorrow, I sit for a live interview on an important public affairs radio program. I am still not a multi-millionaire or household name. But a "public intellectual," sharing my knowledge and ideas with audiences beyond my campus and my small professional community: yes, I am one of those.

As I continue to move toward my goals, I rely on the UA tools*: I record my time, imperfectly, unevenly and sometimes unhappily. I am still working on a format that works well for me. I have a sponsor with whom I rigorously work the steps and from whom I take suggestions. I attend meetings regularly. I have a home meeting where I am getting to know people through outreach calls and their repeated shares. To use the tool of service, I volunteer to chair meetings when I can; I currently have two, once-a-month, commitments at meetings I care about. One of the meetings is specifically for artists and aspiring artists, including writers. I have infrequent action meetings, but I do have them when something is troubling me. I practice possession consciousness by letting go of clothing that doesn't fit or look good anymore, and by dropping projects and obligations that are not serving my needs. I practice the tool of savings by transferring funds automatically from each paycheck to my Individual Retirement Account. I sustain my spiritual life: I continue to pray with coreligionists and say five prayers each morning before rising, the Serenity Prayer, Third Step Prayer, Seventh Step Prayer, and the UA version of the Set-Aside Prayer, plus a religious prayer. I meditate regularly, as part of my yoga practice and in twenty-minute sittings with a recorded guided meditation. I journal most weekdays, a tool I had neglected for many years but returned to at my sponsor's suggestion. Finally, I have an action partner to whom I speak for fifteen minutes every weekday, except when one of us has an unmovable conflict. Since there is a lot of flux in my schedule, I send her a time plan for the following day each evening. I include a paragraph or two of thoughts on how the current day went, and whether I accomplished what I set out to accomplish. Every day, I find something I meant to do but failed to do, some way in which I misread my time and fell behind. I learn from those mistakes. But they don't bother me too much. My life and recovery continue to move forward.

*Editors' Note: For more on the UA Tools:

1. Time Recording – *We must be conscious of how we spend our time. We keep a written record to increase awareness and support our focus on goals and the actions required to achieve them.*
2. Meetings – *We attend UA meetings regularly to share our experience, strength, and hope in order to help ourselves and others recover from underearning.*
3. Sponsorship – *We actively seek sponsorship with someone who has worked the Twelve Steps in UA and is willing to guide us in our recovery.*
4. Possession Consci*ousness – We routinely discard what no longer serves us in order to foster a belief that life is plentiful and that we will be able to provide ourselves with what we need.*
5. Service – *Giving service is vital to our recovery. It is through service to others, and to the Fellowship, that we keep what has been so generously given to us.*
8. Action Partner – *We connect regularly with action partners regarding earning concerns in order to provide each other with accountability, continuity, and support.*
12. Savings - *Saving money demonstrates faith in the future and acceptance of the fact that money is a tool vital to our prosperous vision. We create and follow a savings plan on whatever scale we are able*

Chapter Eleven

The Energy of Yes

Heather in Recovery

My disease says "No" to everything. (UA Symptom 2. *Idea Deflection- We compulsively reject ideas that could expand our lives or careers and increase our profitability.*) Even someone going into the kitchen to make a cup of tea will garner a "no" from me. I used to think I did this because I didn't want to be a burden, but now I realize I am uncomfortable with receiving—anything. So how can my Higher Power relieve me of the burden of underearning, if I won't even accept a cup of tea?

Years ago, before UA even existed, my sponsor in another money program helped me address this issue. I was struggling with the idea of even having a vision. How could I want something or deserve anything? Wasn't that self-will run riot? "Not necessarily," she explained. "If you ask, say: 'Higher Power if it's okay with you…' and then state your need or desire, you will have invited your Higher Power in to grant you that need or desire."

I was still full of doubt. "But how do I know it's my Higher Power's will?" I asked. (Step 3: *Made a decision to turn our will and our lives over the care of God as we understood God*)

"Because you just prayed, 'Higher Power if it's okay with you…'" It sounded way too easy. "If you have asked your Higher Power to guide your thoughts and actions, then your next thought or action will be directed by your Higher Power," she reminded me. "That's what the AA Big Book tells us."

My fear of receiving was so deeply entrenched in my fear of being— visible, who I am meant to be, prosperous, loved—that I couldn't trust my higher power to help me become prosperous or feel loved and successful. "No" was the roadblock to self-acceptance and self-realization.

The thing is that I can turn it over and ask a thousand times and still not see my visions come into my life. I used to think that that meant I was working a bad program, or my Higher Power didn't like me? But what is really going on is that I have said "no" somewhere along the line to my Higher Power's plan. I have blocked the means for my vision to come to me by saying, "No."

We can't see the roadmap or big picture, but our Higher Power can and if direction comes our way and we say, "I don't want to go that way," Higher Power has to find another route. And detours can take years! Believe me!

I am a writer. For 25 years I have wanted to write a best-selling book. I have prayed about this goal and taken loads of actions. I stopped debting. I got a master's degree in creative writing. I wrote several books. I worked the 12-steps with a sponsor. Every summer on the beach, a friend of mine would say, "You should write a book about my aunt." And I would say? "Nah, I don't want to write about that subject."

Meanwhile, I was told by several professional writers to return to the subject of my first book. But I didn't want to write about that subject, again. I said, "No" and remained stuck.

It was when I found UA that I realized that my vision and my Higher Power's vision were not in sync. Why? Because I wasn't listening to what HP wanted me to do. I was saying "No" to the subject Higher Power wanted me to write about. How could I have my vision for a best-selling book, if I kept saying, No? When I finally said, Yes, my life and career changed. It wasn't easy. It took a lot of time and energy, but I wrote the book. It has been heralded as "my masterpiece;" it has sold all over the world and I have received two prestigious awards for my work. More importantly, the book allowed me to be of service to the world and raise awareness of two issues close to my heart—women's rights and human rights. It also prepared the path for my next book—on the same subject—which I am writing now: the book about my friend's aunt that I have spent the past 25 years saying "No" to writing!

How much easier would my life have been if I had said "Yes" when Higher Power presented the idea the first time.

Saying "Yes" facilitates Higher Power's activity in my life and my career. My ability to be of service is also deeply connected to the energy of Yes. I say Yes to projects now. Now when I pray, "Higher Power if it is okay with you, I would like..." and state my heart's desire. Then I add, "And while we're at it, what is the next thing you want me to do?" The guidance is not always something I want to do, but I trust my Higher Power now, and respond (most of the time) with an enthusiastic "Yes!"

PART FIVE

Changing Ourselves, Evolving our Program and Our Relationships

Chapter Twelve

The Queen Comes Home: A Very Imperfect Arrival

Emma from Oregon

This isn't the essay I expected to write about what recovery has done for me, yet in another sense, the forthcoming words are no surprise at all. Maybe they express my having "finally arrived" -- my having reached a destination that I'd long convinced myself was a pipe dream. I'm now into year seven of financial recovery, but I'm far from a millionaire. My financial resources today are at their lowest ebb in years, and I'm barely a "thousand-aire" at the moment. My seven-years-ago self would've wanted to hear that by now he's a billionaire. Then he'd at last be protected from life. Un-shameable. Or so he thought.

Fifteen minutes before sitting at my computer to tell this story tonight, I had an unwelcome experience that shows how far I've come. As I was walking up my own one-lane street, an older man rolled down the window of his faded SUV as he was driving by, stopped, looked me in the eyes and said, "God you're attractive -- f***ing faggot!" And then drove off, probably to a house within blocks of mine. Today I can admit that I am frightened to the core, powerless, and confused by the state of the world and of my world. I can step away from useless self-blame as well. I accept that I can't do life alone. I accept that maybe I'm facing terrifying opposition not because I'm wrong but because I'm daring to shine. For the first time in my life, I am being openly visible as my authentic self before an ever-widening circle of people. What started tentatively with just a few folks in anonymous online forums and twelve-step phone lines is now spilling out on YouTube and Instagram.

Seven years ago, I couldn't imagine coming out to the world -- or my family -- as anything so controversial as trans-woman. I couldn't imagine dealing with the ramifications of that while also having just been fired from a job, as happened in July. Today I'm still struggling with a deep bitterness about being financially vulnerable once again, to the point of questioning whether recovery works at all. The breakthrough, the sign to me that I'm going to get through this, however, is that I can say that to you. I can tell you how I feel about it and acknowledge I'm not sure what to do beyond the apparent "next right action." Before recovery I was so dissociated from my own experience that the only emotion I could name was fear. Fear had been there all the time, supposedly because that's how I deserved to live. Any other feelings I had were the ones I thought others would consider convenient for me to have. Anger was self-indulgent. I was American, so I didn't have shame. Under those conditions I was necessarily very alone and without direction.

Though I seemingly didn't have shame, shame was running my life: family relations; finances; my litany of dead-end, abusive and underpaying jobs; and what few friendships I had. Shame was keeping me secretive and small. I'd inwardly dreamt of being some kind of star since childhood and had notions of a personal destiny where I became a transformative public figure whose brilliant ideas inspired the brightest people in the world. To my credit, many people were convinced of my genius. Fifth-grade aptitude tests showed I was reading like a college senior. When I was twelve years old, an uncle read one of my science fiction stories and declared it more brilliant than much of what he saw from professional colleagues. This uncle had written much of the *Batman* and *All in the Family* TV series.

Nevertheless, I compulsively cringed when anyone came anywhere near me with a camera. I broke out in a cold sweat when I saw my name in print. And I beat myself up for all the cringing. How would I become a public figure when I reacted like this? I was an idiot for having dreams at all, and if I needed convincing, I just had to conjure Dad's voice. If only I could start some cutting-edge business, become a real-estate mogul or go on some never-before-attempted globe-trotting adventure, I could prove Dad wrong.

I ran endless programs on myself to pull myself up by my bootstraps: diets, workouts, self-help books, seminars using relentless discipline. I went to financial planners and business coaches I couldn't afford, settling shamefacedly for their freebies. I became a minor leader working 120-hour weeks for an organization that promised I'd become a Gandhi-level world leader if I enrolled enough people in their courses. I tried mens' weekends, real-estate courses and multi-level marketing schemes only to become paralyzed when they talked about "action." While my fear that women found me creepy was spectacularly confirmed on a number of occasions, the story in my head was probably worse than the reality most of the time. So, I had a go at sleazy pick-up artist courses, only to find my throat locking up when I got a passing glance from a woman whom beer commercials said to like. I had a vague idea that therapy might make a difference someday, but I didn't dare such self-indulgence. I was "fine." I wanted to open up to people but didn't know how. By age 35, I didn't believe a word I said. That year I graduated with a Master's degree from a leading architecture school. Then my life imploded along with the US banking system, and I spent the next two years living in my childhood bedroom, penniless, writing a business plan for the latest billion-dollar venture and meditating on the wordless tension and financial panic that exuded from the walls of my mother's house.

Today I'm reeling from a hate incident, bitter about yet another job search, and dealing once again with financial anxiety. But what's different is that I don't have to face it alone, and I don't have anything to hide. In 2012, I found my way to Debtors Anonymous, then Underearners Anonymous shortly after. By then I was living in a community house to which I'd given hundreds of hours of unsolicited free work. At the same time, I was four months behind in rent. Working my programs, I became willing to take any job, paid off the debt, made my way to Oregon, and after a couple of rough years hustling any way, I could, I found myself working as an assistant on contract for a freelance web developer, let's call him "S." During my first three years working for S, I was busy. Our working relationship was easy and fun, and he paid me fairly well. In many ways I had an ideal situation -- I could make my own schedule, pay my bills on 20-hour workweeks, and sic my big brain on challenging problems for a portfolio of loyal clients whom I didn't have to find. A couple of years in, I was S's expert developer. I built up some savings, and many of my recovery action partners noted S was getting an incredible deal for his money. They encouraged me to negotiate for more.

Around the beginning of the fourth year, S realized he was burning out. We discussed my taking the business over, but he kept cancelling our transition meetings and let the business fall apart. Our communication became bilaterally avoidant. He began paying my invoices weeks, then months late. I now had enough recovery to be willing to see what was happening, and with the help of numerous pressure relief groups, action groups, outreach calls and meetings across 2018 I prayed for S to find his true vocation, while I laid the groundwork for my own freelance web development business. I rented a shared office, built an exquisite website, and was soon offering expert consultation for $100/hour. I could see that I was really earning less than minimum wage because I was tracking my time and money (Editors' Note: UA Tool 1. *Time Recording – We must be conscious of how we spend our time. We keep a written record to increase awareness and support our focus on goals and the actions required to achieve them.* DA Tool 2. Record Maintenance *We maintain records of our daily income and expenses, of our savings, and of the retirement of any portions of our outstanding debts.*)

I was making hundreds of cold calls but getting only tiny projects for difficult clients that were hardly worth the effort. My money fellowships taught me to diligently get half-payment up front, but I was chasing clients for their second installments over months. Working with a business coach, I came to see that I was marketing to everyone, and thereby marketing to no-one. By the end of 2018, I had $500 left of the $15,000 savings I'd had the year before, and I was so emotionally fried that I couldn't bring myself to show up at the office. With the help of my recovery team, I finally became willing to ask a question I thought only others were allowed to ask: If I win at this, will I be happy? Well, no! Supposedly this business was there to support the "frivolous" hobby projects that I really wanted to be devoting my life to. Really, I'd taken it on so once again I'd have a respectable front to hide behind. It was terrifying to admit that my heart wasn't in it.

Meanwhile as a part of my step work, I was working a "searching and fearless moral inventory" of my sexual behavior. (Editors' Note: UA Step 4) This inventory revealed that while traditional religion might call gender nonconformity a sin, I'd been "sinning" for decades by hiding who I was. In my last couple of years of recovery, therapy, and ever more daring cosplay in the safe spaces of ecstatic dance and the local kink scene, I'd begun suspecting that I might be transgender -- that under my shabby, shy boy facade lived a brilliant, playful queen, a born performance artist with a fiery wit and epic fashion sense. I was hurting people by hiding her in desk jobs. By chasing women to prove my manhood, I was only scaring women. I was worrying friends and family with decades of non-dating. I was the party pooper and the guy who'd insert himself into a lusty conversation between a girl and another guy, secretly working to ensure he didn't "get any." I wasn't letting myself anywhere near the vibrant LGBTQIA community in my city, terrified of my long-dead father. I freaked a number of drag queens out with my desperate window-shopping and secret longing, standing frozen at their tables after their performances, too petrified to utter a word. I couldn't market myself because that meant promoting a false identity. I was left to either live on crumbs or become dependent on non-consenting others. The Bible might say what it says about men and women, but my higher power was demanding I step boldly into who I really am.

With a lot of prayer and meditation, I admitted to my sponsor that the career I thought I was building was dead. I became willing to take a full-time job to recuperate. The job that came was underpaid, but it was a miracle. As a tech-support agent in a call center, I was fielding complex user issues for a superstar internet company for $13 an hour. Underpaid or not, my nerves were grateful for the check, regular schedule, health benefits and office camaraderie. This was like the fun version of high-school I'd never experienced, where I got to be that playful queen every day. I discovered a hugely popular YouTube channel that showed me what might be possible if I took the stage as my true self, as I'd secretly dreamed. I knew going in that my little job could be as temporary or as permanent as I wanted it to be, that it could be a safe harbor for incubating my potential as a content-creating performer. I now wonder if my Higher Power has been secretly training me for being a public figure after all. All those "qualification" shares in twelve-step rooms? The cosplay at ecstatic dances? Even the "enrollment" conversations in that cultish organization? Yep, prep for the airwaves. I can see that since I've been "out," I've been effortlessly creating fans everywhere I go. While at the job I came out as trans to my family, on social media, and on YouTube with a first video that's gotten rave reviews. My camera shyness has become camera gluttony. I'm starting to make waves in the local drag scene. I've turned one of my hobby coding projects into a successful art exhibition.

But in the midst of all these results, I also got fired from that job. Statistically I was one of the best performing agents, but I didn't handle a couple of emotionally triggering calls well, and policy is policy. My old self would have spiraled into self-blame, and I have had to deal with a whirlwind of anxiety and bitterness since it happened. Much of the time, I've been unwilling to go through another job search, and have had to accept even that unwillingness, turning it over to my Higher Power. And then, just tonight, there was this hate incident right in front of my house.

Hence, my talk of "arrival." I've learned in recovery that none of us finishes life alive and that's ok. I am once again quaking in fear though I'm safe in my apartment, have food in the fridge, have loving friendships, have renewed relations with my family, and even a little money in the bank. I now know that there's magic and power in being positively visible, in sharing how I feel, even when I feel terrible. I no longer feel guilty for taking up space. Instead of blaming myself, I accept that the job may not have been a fit -- I am a highly sensitive personality. My sensitivity is not a weakness; it's just the other side of intelligence. Rather than try to dull this capacity, I've become interested in environments where it's an asset. From what I can figure, I make a better performance artist than corporate accountant, and why fight it? Taking my transgenderism as a metaphor for everything else in my life, I only hurt myself and others by trying to be what I was never meant to be. I'm starting to trust that my Higher Power will work with me if I get out of the way, and that I can trust it with my nastiest shames and secrets. In that spirit, I'm turning the bitterness that has me at times unwilling to track my time and numbers at all into a fun YouTube video that I hope will inspire hundreds, if not thousands of people. I recognize that the hate incident isn't about me, and it's only clarified the reality around the country and world I live in, without any sugar-coating. My "queen" has already reached out to the local newspaper with a letter that invites the perpetrator to a sane discussion. I've outreached to local leaders about how we might make the neighborhood safer for everyone. Today's been a hard day. But taking it one breath at a time, I accept that I am where I need to be.

Chapter Thirteen

From Surviving the Symptoms to Prosperity and Recovery

Clare in Australia

I was in a 12-step program for substance addiction for over twenty years. When attending meetings, I felt utterly miserable. Even the newest newcomer seemed to be working and earning in a career of some kind or had travelled overseas. This was not the recovery I had signed up for. It was getting harder to say that life was better in sobriety. I had thrived in some areas of my life but not in terms of career or earning. As my disease progressed, it started to impact those other areas of my life that were doing well such as parenting and family. I was weighed down by crippling debt and had been in severe financial hardship for over a decade. I had no prospects for any of the dreams I had in mind, I wanted to work and earn as a creative in art or design. I had lost all hope.

Before coming to UA, money as well as debt came into my household via my husband. I also received government assistance at various times. I worked unskilled jobs requiring no qualifications such as cleaning. I was a stay-at-home mother, a fulltime student, and several times a part-time student. I had some success as a practicing artist, but this was dogged with underearning, under-being and misusing opportunities. I was unable to get or allow the support from others that I craved. I obtained graphic design skills but again my disease rendered me unable to use these skills to make money. I never felt qualified enough for any position advertised and found negotiating and working as a freelancer to be extremely uncomfortable because of symptoms such as undervaluing or underpricing, misplaced guilt and shame and needing to prove my worth and value. (Editors' Note: UA Symptom 7: *Undervaluing and Under-pricing – We undervalue our abilities and services and fear asking for increases in compensation or for what the market will bear.* UA Symptom 10: *Misplaced Guilt or Shame – We feel uneasy when asking for or being given what we need or what we are owed.* UA Symptom 3: Compulsive *Need to Prove – Although we have demonstrated competence in our jobs or business, we are driven by a need to re-prove our worth and value.*) My decisions became something I severely regretted over and again, as getting my foot in the door became even harder to obtain. I was diagnosed as being severely depressed. Entering the workplace became an insurmountable hurdle. I unwittingly, fed into negative theories and beliefs about earning and achieving and the capabilities I needed or lacked. In the end, feeling so unworthy, I believed that the only rational path was to accept any crumbs left over. The disease centered in my ongoing obsession of how to solve the issue of work and money.

Right before my recovery from underearning, I was working in unskilled disability care work which was unrelated to my qualifications. I exhibited the symptom of stability boredom here most of all and resented the time I was spending there. (Editors' Note: UA Symptom 12: *Stability Boredom – We create unnecessary conflict with co-workers, supervisors and clients, generating problems that result in financial distress.*) Doing a job I felt I hated and at the same time feeling guilty for being so ungrateful was very painful. I could have prospered if I was there to serve others or myself. I was only there for the low wage.

Through members, I found Debtors Anonymous and understood instantly that I was an underearner. I felt, "if only I had a problem of overspending or mismanagement of money," at least there would be a solution. I could not "earn" money without underbeing and feeling miserable; when I did, the amount was very little. When I found out about Underearners Anonymous, I continued to keep my numbers, a tool of D.A. but transferred to working the steps in UA as my underearning situation was intensifying. (Editors' Note: DA Tool 2: *Record Maintenance We maintain records of our daily income and expenses, of our savings, and of the retirement of any portions of our outstanding debts.*) I had quit my job and was in worse financial shape than when I came into DA. In Underearners Anonymous I learned that I had an addiction to underearning which included suffering. In active addiction, I degraded myself for money.

When I read about time indifference, and giving away my time, I felt hope. (Editors' Note: UA Symptom 1: *Time Indifference – We put off what must be done and do not use our time to support our own vision and further our own goals.*) I was elated to discover that I identified with every symptom. I felt that I could be really good at this. With recovery, I would have something to give. In the past, people either did not ask me to sponsor them or if I did, it was short lived and I questioned my ability to be of service. (Editors' Note: UA Tool 3 *Sponsorship – We actively seek sponsorship with someone who has worked the Twelve Steps in UA and is willing to guide us in our recovery.*) In UA I have had a lot of requests for sponsorship. I have taken eight people through all or most of the 12 steps. I currently sponsor three people and have experienced all of the benefits that come with those relationships.

After beginning the program and working with a UA sponsor. I was able to return to the workplace I left, practice gratitude and learn how to be a worker amongst workers. After a time, it became feasible for me to work with my husband, and I created a company. Because of the disease of underearning, such collaboration would have been impossible before UA. We expanded from new home sales into the broader realm of real estate. Over the past six years in UA, we have paid off over $91,391.00 worth of personal debt and our company made over six figures for two years running including a profit one year.

When our industry suffered a downturn with two thirds leaving the industry and seeking alternative employment or further study, I too went back to my old job in disability care, which remained a very, very poor environment for me. Because of the new way I was able to show up as a recovered person, I earned a promotion. I also found I was becoming depressed, so I sought professional help. I was suffering for money again, but I learned in UA that life is more than money. Consequently, with love and support, I am spending my remaining years on the planet using my gifts and talents. In doing so, I am able to best serve others and the planet.

I have a talent for running a business and being creative. I am back in real estate and selling new homes as well as making art. I am grateful I can work and earn without being motivated by fear and self-seeking. As a result, we almost made six figures and have been steadily improving ever since.

A long slow recovery is best for me in UA. I initially thought that tough words, tough love, discipline and hard work were what I needed to recover. Instead, I need to slow down, take time and be at peace. I have a new relationship with time. An understanding that recovery and things take time, I don't feel the need to rush, panic, solve or to know how to do something that needs to be learned or practiced. As an underearner I need to work the program on a daily basis, otherwise, this disease can and will kill me.

My obsession with ideas about how I could make money or sell my work as a creative took up more time than making the work. I was actually not very good at BE-ing a creative. I did not put time into practicing my craft. I became more concerned with catching up, making money, and achieving success or recognition. Before I found UA, I had decided I would be satisfied if I was just able to do good work. Before UA I treated art as a hobby; in recovery, I have been more consistent with my creative practice than ever before. Prosperity in my life comes from having the freedom to be my own boss, and self-care such as going out more, spending time in nature, having fun and connecting with others. It also means taking care of my physical and mental health, and this works by putting my spiritual health in the program first.

I have been instrumental in starting a meeting that allowed myself and others to attend without a time change. I have contact with people, locally, interstate and around the world. UA is a "we" program. I need other people, a small village of recovery. Regularly attending a home group is one way to do this. People I am drawn to and that give me joy are to be embraced. My old belief was that I cannot maintain these relationships and that they would tire of me. This was part of my under-being.

My sponsor always re-affirms self-love and acceptance. I am learning to ask, "how is this serving me?" with more love each day. UA is a daily program of action for me, the biggest action being connection with self and a God of my understanding.

I still make my own choices but with the support of other people. I no longer believe there is a certain road I should be on and that I am not on it. I am still driven to create things whether they make money or not. I am here and unique and have survived my life so far. I have permission to let go of struggle and concern. I pursue my life with the absence of fear and self-seeking with the help of a high power.

Chapter Fourteen

From Debt and Deprivation to Peace and Prosperity

Jennifer from California

Thirty-five years ago, I joined my first 12-step program. I am now in four, two of which deal with financial recovery. I came into the first of those in a panic about money needed for a car repair. I also owed my parents money, and through that program, I managed the car repair and repaid the debt. I then left the program, only to return a year later in worse debt and more despair. That was in 1999. I added the other financial recovery program in 2014. The combination transformed my financial life from vagueness to clarity, lack to abundance, and little attention to rigorous management. My poverty thinking also shifted to prosperity consciousness; my low self-esteem changed to feelings of self-worth, self-acceptance, and personal empowerment. My life is now filled with peace, nourishing relationships, and a loving higher power—my best source of wisdom, strength, and serenity.

What created this transformation, and how do I maintain and continue to grow in prosperity?

I first took the 12 steps, and I now live them. I got a sponsor at a meeting, (Editors' Note: UA Tool 3 *Sponsorship - We actively seek sponsorship with someone who has worked the Twelve Steps in UA and is willing to guide us in our recovery.*) did assignments on the steps which she gave me and read those to her. We mostly used the Alcoholics Anonymous Big Book for guidance with working the steps. We didn't go through the steps on a schedule, but as I finished my assignments. I continue to practice the program principles, and this spiritual process of healing creates inner changes in me which produce the outer transformation in my finances.

On a daily basis, I pray for God's will, meditate for guidance and renewal, and seek to be of service. Somedays, it's giving a smile, and others, it's listening to a fellow, with acceptance and support. I have a monthly spending and earning plan, which is a Debtors Anonymous (DA) program tool. (Editors' Note: DA Tool 5. Spending Plan: *The spending plan puts our needs first and gives us clarity and balance in our spending. It includes categories for income, spending, debt payment, and savings (to help us build cash reserves, however humble*). The income plan helps us focus on increasing our income. The debt payment category guides us in making realistic payment arrangements without depriving ourselves. Savings can include prudent reserve, retirement, and special purchases. I developed it on my own and with input from others in Pressure Relief Meetings, which are other program tools. (Editors' Note: DA Tool 4. Pressure Relief Groups and Pressure Relief Meetings *After we have gained some familiarity with the D.A. program, we organize Pressure Relief Groups consisting of ourselves and two other recovering debtors who have not incurred unsecured debt for at least 90 days and who usually have more experience in the program. The group meets in a series of Pressure Relief Meetings to review our financial situation. These meetings typically result in the formulation of a spending plan and an action plan.*) I record everything that I spend and earn daily, total at the end of each week and month, and plan for the next month. It's objective and brings clarity. I keep up-to-date with my financial accounts: savings, checking, investments, and credit card.

I've also focused on building my savings and investments for many years. Some of the money came from an inheritance and some from some workers compensation settlements, but most of it came from my work earnings. I started these financial programs without this money, and now, through working my programs and the grace of God, I have a substantial level of funds in my accounts. This has brought me great peace amidst changing economic times. The amount has gone up and down over the years, but the overall trajectory has been up. This has been miraculous for me because I used to be suicidal and lay awake at night, anxious about how I was going to survive financially.

I also have a financial planner who is savvy and careful with his management of my finances. I got the advisor on a recommendation from a friend who used his services and had great success with his money. Since investments are not my expertise, I got the planner to best manage the funds. I work to be a good steward of this money and all my possessions, including myself and anything else under my direction. Everything I am and have belongs to God, and I am their caretaker.

I am also committed to being solvent. I got out of debt in 1999 and have stayed out of debt. I paid one debt off in a lump sum, and I paid the other off in installments and then as a lump sum once it was at a manageable amount. My spiritual practice is that I remain solvent and debt-free. If an expense is not manageable, I don't do it—no matter what. For purchases I'm uncertain about, sometimes the answer is "no" to buying it, and for others, I either have the money, or God provides it in an unforeseen way. For instance, I recently needed a new refrigerator, and I got an unexpected check for $700. I then bought a new one for $856.04. The store also gave me a $100 credit for a previous delivery issue. Thus, thanks to my higher power's $800 gift, the new refrigerator just cost $56.04.

I've remained solvent through my highest earning jobs to months-long periods of no work, without unemployment insurance. Debt is deadly. It's a rock weighing one down, like a fake intimate relationship. It's always there, and even though it's uncomfortable, it's a familiar attachment, so letting that go leaves an emptiness, which needs filling. Program practices, such as being of service to others, connecting with God and loving friends in and outside of program, using my creative gifts and other nurturing activities are more satisfying attachments, which now fill my life.

Time is another possession which I honor. I plan and record my time, which is an Underearners Anonymous (UA) program tool. (Editors' Note: UA Tool 1 Time Recording – *We must be conscious of how we spend our time. We keep a written record to increase awareness and support our focus on goals and the actions required to achieve them.*) It helps me manage my finances and other parts of my life in an efficient and productive way. I don't set myself up for stress and failure by planning 20 tasks for a day. I set myself up for success and choose one or a few must do's, and leave space for the unexpected, which derails the best organized plan. Life is like a movie, where I must adapt when the scene changes.

I give service in my various groups, whether it's using the tool* of communication and supporting others in a kind text or call or sharing my story to offer hope and tools for living in health and freedom. (Editors' Note: UA Tool 10. Communication – *We contact other UA members to seek support, to diminish isolation, and to reinforce our commitments to action.*) Service is win-win, nurturing the giver and receiver. I take outreach calls to support others in their recovery, speak and give service in meetings, and I sponsor and guide others with step-work. (Editors' Note: UA Tool: 5. Service – *Giving service is vital to our recovery. It is through service to others, and to the Fellowship, that we keep what has been so generously given to us.*) I also read spiritual literature from my faith and programs. My favorite program literature is the AA Big Book, since it is the primary text with the original instructions for 12-step recovery. (Editors' Note: *11. Literature – We read UA Conference Approved Literature to strengthen our understanding of this compulsive disease and the process of recovery.*) I wake up to it in the morning and end my day with it at night. It guides me to live a God-filled and directed day.

I see life through God's eyes now instead of just my own. Thanks to having a mind free of financial toil, I see God's presence all around. I see it in the squirrels, which dart up-and-down the tree outside my window, the love of my friends, and the sunsets, which inspire me to awe. What about the hard times, though? As I am writing this the world is sheltering-at-home due to the coronavirus. As a substitute teacher, I am at home since the schools are closed, and I'm collecting unemployment. The day I learned that the schools were closing, I applied for unemployment. I acted on my behalf right away. After being in recovery for many years, I have learned that I am valuable, and I advocate for myself as my normal course of action.

I had difficulty getting three weeks of benefits because I had a three-week penalty with unemployment for something that occurred three years ago. I called my state assemblyman for help. He had a contact at the unemployment office, who told me that I could appeal the three-week penalty. I did and won the appeal. I was eligible to receive the rest of the benefits, too, since I paid into unemployment insurance and met the requirements for it.

With the pandemic, though, I am one with others across the planet, not knowing what will happen tomorrow or in the distant future. Will schools reopen in the fall? Will they be online or partly online? Will they need substitutes? They don't know. Thus, I cry when strong feelings hit and sometimes shake in panic. I then reach out to loving people for comfort and guidance, pray, and put the matter in my God box. This practice brings me peace.

I've also applied for other work and have continued to apply. I do this on my own, and sometimes, I commit this task to an action partner and bookend later to say what I completed. I'm responsible for taking action, and then I let go and trust God. He always sees me through and helps me grow wiser and stronger from each challenge.

Living this blend of practical steps and spiritual connection has given me the courage and freedom to attain some life visions. To develop my faith, I meditate once or twice a day, do the "Nightly Review" on Page 86 in the AA Big Book at night, and I go through the "Upon Awakening" section on Pages 86-88 in the Big Book when I get up in the morning. With the strong base of faith, many visions have come true, such as having two books published.

I also spent 2½ years traveling, mostly internationally. I went to places, such as Egypt, Russia, Alaska, and Australia. Each trip was life-changing, and although I greatly revere academia and love academic study, traveling gave me the best education. There is no replacement for walking the streets of a country and talking to natives to learn about a people and their culture. I worked with my financial planner to manage these trips solvently. I got clarity on my travel vision through listening to people share on the UA Prosperous Travel Vision meeting, talking to people from that meeting, listening to my inner desires, and talking to travel agents.

What does attaining visions have to do with money? It is life beyond financial struggle. I came into these programs doing little to care for myself and nurture my soul and cultural interests. Now, I frequently do activities which I love, such as going to plays and musicals. I used to get the worst tickets, since they were the cheapest. Now, I am still prudent with my spending, but I choose better seats, which are financially manageable and give a more enjoyable experience of the performance. My friends are happier, too, with the better seats.

I also buy healthier food, such as salmon and papaya. I'm worth it. I went from no self-esteem and feeling like a gnat on the floor, to being a woman who opens her arms wide to the abundance of the universe. Love and prosperity overflow from me to others, for these gifts aren't just for me; they're for everyone. This all came from working my four programs diligently, doing the steps, continuing to work them all in earnest, and helping others. I take all this very seriously, and I work my programs as though my life depends upon it, because it surely does. Without doing my programs, the result could be a physical death or living as a "dead" person, not being my true self and living a full life.

Pain still comes in life, such as the stress from the pandemic. Eventually, the crisis will pass. Society will be different, and even though my stomach sometimes tightens in fear, I relax knowing that God is here, storms pass, and sunnier days will come.

My financial world is a sunny part of my life now. It used to be a dark volcano, of which I felt ashamed. Today, I am grateful that I live a healthy, prosperous life and have a beautiful condominium on a golf course. Coincidentally, after my father passed away, family and friends bought a bench with his name on it, which is on the golf course near where I live. It was one of God's gifts, which fills my life.

Recently, a dream told me to "keep my eyes on the prize." What is the prize? My prize is to connect with God and follow his will. This brings peace, for as Dante wrote in the *Divine Comedy*, "In his will is our peace"

God is first in my life and seeking to live in a manner pleasing to him is my focus. One such area is living a healthy financial life, and I support others in doing the same. Our how-to's and numbers may differ, but the practical steps and spiritual support, which we can access, are the same. Many years ago, I told someone that I was "bad" with money. He told me that I was "good" with money. I then started affirming that I was good with money. Twenty-six years after starting my financial recovery, I am good with money. I showed up, did the work, and persisted on the path.

I am grateful for my life of financial manageability, peace, and prosperity. It's brought me a life of service, meaning, and contribution. Healing and recovery are possible for all.

Chapter Fifteen

A Different Recovery

Anonymous in Anonymous

He Didn't Hear His Higher Power in Meetings, but in Working with Others, Higher Power Appeared

If I tell my story clearly, I am probably lymy ing.

(Wow, that wasn't what I typed; the computer genies have played tricks with my words already.)

If I tell my story clearly, I am probably lying.

If I tell it vaguely, I am telling the truth. But then you won't understand. I hope that Spirit gives me the words to find the right balance. This is my story. Or maybe it's a poem.

A snake brushed my foot. I was sponsoring, and four snakes came out from the edge of the lawn where I lived, across the grass—I am not afraid of snakes, and in fact, I love them—and then one of them brushed my bare foot. They were black, graceful, and wise. Their eyes were calm and without hate. I knew I was blessed; I was honored by Nature, I was neither condemned nor abandoned; I was not judged unworthy of help, spiritual or tangible; there was not one more box to check before I could be loved. I could not deny what I had seen and felt. It was only a moment; then the snakes slithered off, but I was changed. The change was on the inside even more than on the outside, but my outside changed too.

For you, change may not come through an encounter with snakes. Your change agent might not even be an animal. I have no idea, absolutely anything could ignite your change. I thought I knew what recovery would be for someone other than myself, but I don't; I only sort of know my own experience, and somewhere down inside myself I know my own story. So, I hope you won't assume your story has to be similar to mine in the specifics—only my relationship to my story equals your relationship to your story.

Was I such a great sponsor? Did I sponsor harder than anyone? No. [Editors' note: *UA Tool 3 Sponsorship: We actively seek sponsorship with someone who has worked to Twelve Steps in UA and is willing to guide us in our recovery*] Did I work the Steps, the Tools, the Traditions, extra tools I had heard about from some person sharing in a meeting? Sometimes I did some of those last things-- a neurotic, paranoid tendency of mine, I have learned. But that isn't what earned me miracles. I had miracles in spite of these things, not because of them. I showed up to sponsor, not really expecting I was going to do a great job, but knowing gently, inside, that somehow it would be OK. All I had to do was try and that would be enough. And I *could* try.

In sponsoring I had a level playing field for the first time. My effort was enough. Before that, doing *more* than what I could do was what I always thought necessary. (Editors' note: *UA Symptom 3:*

Compulsive Need to Prove: Although we demonstrated competence in our jobs or business, we are driven by a need to re-prove our worth and value.) And it would never be enough, so I learned I had to try even harder. Exertion, exhaustion, collapse, more exertion.

Going to meetings hadn't helped me that much. I never really heard MY conception of God in the rooms—I always thought others had a different God than mine, and others had more self-discipline than I did. As a disabled person, suffering from a physical and mental chronic, infectious illness, I believed I was f**ked. And anyway, my fellow travelers were all sitting in a circle talking, as if that was how to recover, how to get help from Spirit—not doing ritual, which was what I conceived and had experienced as how to communicate with and get help from Higher Power. My conception of God was one developed in a spiritual community and with a teacher from another culture entirely, so different from the one I grew up in. It was in community, doing ritual, in nature, that I had an experience of spirit that let me feel complete, loved, supported, enough—and resulted in $60,000 arriving in my life out of the blue. That allowed me to travel to another continent, where my teacher had grown up, a deeply moving pilgrimage, and to survive off the money until I hit a bottom.

I didn't hear my conception of God in the meetings, I didn't see it in jobs, and I lost it when I wasn't with my community anymore.

But that changed when I sponsored—now I didn't need talking in a circle, nor for others to be willing or understanding of how to do a ritual with me, nor for a sponsor to make miracles happen for me. How had I gotten there?

—

The first day, my sponsor told me working with others works when all else fails. He said:

Meetings	may fail
[Action meetings]	may fail
Prayer and meditation	may fail
Conversations	may fail

Working with others works when all else fails.

I said, "All else is failing, how about now?" He said, "go ahead;" he said something like, "you sponsor when you need to, not when you think you're ready."

That set me free. Somehow, I knew I was ready. And I needed to. I had said I didn't know what the hell I was doing, but in my gut I felt serenity knowing that I would be given power to do what I needed to do.

My first time sponsoring, as I walked toward the place where I was going to sit in the park to speak by mobile phone, I felt a wind behind me. Not a physical wind, but a wind of Spirit. It was like the ancestors were back, the spirits that had given me so much strength in the past. While I was sitting there reading from the *Big Book* with my sponsee, I noticed little green bugs sitting on my pants, and on my Big Book, wrapping me in a blanket of support.

It had taken four years for me to get a sponsor. Well, That's kind of a lie. When I first got into this other, money-related program, I got a sponsor right away. But his electricity got turned off, and then my cell phone got lost, and I didn't have any other copy of his phone number. In hindsight, I thought maybe I'd dodged a bullet. So, then I got another sponsor. He was okay, but after a few months, he said he was leaving the program. I envied him, getting to just stop working this program I really didn't want to work. Instead, he got to focus on another program, one I really liked, but thought I couldn't work yet. I thought I needed to work the unpleasant program for my survival. I figured my Higher Power wanted me to work harder in order to earn a sponsor.

I did get a sponsor in that other program that I liked better, though, and he was supportive, but I wasn't sure that he had his money problems solved. In the money-related meetings I kept checking the box that said I was looking for a sponsor on the "We Care" sheet. (There was never any check mark in the "available to sponsor" space.) It took me four years to find my sponsor, but that doesn't mean it has to take you that long. I don't know anyone else's timetable.

I kept trying to get my health back together and made some headway. I got some employment with "recovery jobs"—but whenever I went off my medication, the physical illness came back. Eventually I got laid off again.

A new tool for health came into my life from HP—I can't take credit; my part was merely following my curiosity—and I had a miracle. My doctor wanted me to take heavy-duty drugs, but I was afraid and unwilling. So, I asked Spirit. Spirit told me a prescription—take the pill the doctor recommends for 13 days, then stop for 13 days, then take it for 13, then stop for 13, then take it 13 more. What on Earth did that mean? I wondered. Probably just random noise, and we were just getting gobbledygook. But when I went to the doctor, he said to take the pill for two weeks, go off it for two weeks, take it for two weeks, *etc*. I was stunned. But willing to try, because Spirit had earned my trust. That treatment gave me substantial progress in reclaiming my health. I still wasn't workforce-ready, but I was awed and grateful.

I kept up the B work (Editors' note: *B-Job: a backup job or bridge job that one takes in preparation for one's prosperity job*) for a few more years, attended meetings, and hoping to find a sponsor and not finding one. I would read coaching books that I found inspiring and even life-changing, and tried to offer work as a coach, as a writer, as many other things, but nothing ever took off. I couldn't even give my services away. Maybe I needed formal training?

Instead, yet another new spiritual teaching came into my life, again not through my ingenuity, and not because I was looking. The practice was unadvertised, like the Twelve Step programs, and less well-known which is why I have to give credit to my Higher Power for bringing it to my awareness at all. Someone from another program told me about meetings of people studying this path. She thought the approach was a good fit for the kind of support group I was seeking. The new spiritual teaching opened up vistas that I had not considered. This was *the* most pivotal change of my life.

However, shortly afterward, I hit bottom. Working a job that was truly awful, I contracted a weird infection. Also, I was selling something that went against my values, breaking UA traditions, and losing money. Ironically, I would have been better if I'd just trusted that money was on its way and not done the “responsible” thing. I had this wonderful spiritual tool and meetings that let my spirit soar, even better than ever before, yet I just couldn’t trust the process. I couldn’t hold onto my spiritual connection when needed. Then I got fired from one of the agencies for which I worked part-time. Getting fired drove me to go to an extra meeting that day.

It was there that I got my true sponsor. Someone had actually checked the “available to sponsor” box on the sheet. Although this still wasn't UA, he just happened to be passing the steps on both this other issue and underearning as a unit. I asked him if I could work UA, as that was more my issue, even though I didn't think I had done enough days of solvency perfectly, and he said you're being too perfectionistic, and people need service. So that's when I started going seriously to UA meetings.

However, sponsoring made a more significant change in me. By sponsoring, I got to recognize that a) my sponsor wasn’t my Higher Power (he had told me this many times I’m sure, but it didn’t mean anything until I experienced the truth of it) because I had miracles *even when he wasn’t there to help me*, and b) that I could use all of what had been given to me in the past, all my outside resources, or let them go, without any effort to figure it out. I would know in the moment; I would be guided in every moment. I had a taste of unconditional freedom, whereas before it had always been dependent on some group or teacher outside myself. Now for the first time in my life I was the teacher—and yet miracles were happening!

Gradually I felt more stable, more able to let go and trust. I was gifted a chance to pursue a professional training that could help my health get more fully rebuilt and make me an abundant living. It seemed that a direction was opening up for me in the tangible world as well as in Spirit.

I'd be lying if I said that life is all pleasant and prosperous. And I’d be a real drag if I made it sound like life is lousy, and you should just settle for surviving the disease and not ask for anything more. Life today is a mixed bag, amazing and hard. In fact, at some moments I think I don't have any recovery whatsoever. After some point, even working with others as I’d been doing it lost its charm. I felt called to leverage my service by working on the Literature Committee. I learned many valuable and satisfying things from that experience. And after that became frustrating and full of doubts – because the infrastructure wasn't in place yet to ensure that I wasn't just throwing my work into a void--I took a bit more autonomy and began working on a pamphlet that speaks what I feel is the core of the program. That led to my being asked to contribute my story to this collection which I had had no idea was being assembled. I suppose that's a bit of a miracle. The point is, I believe, God is my employer and has different specific jobs for me. Life in recovery for me is about satisfaction, service, and freedom. It is a mystery, but a clear mystery.

Fear of financial insecurity has left me to quite a degree, although not 100%. I do not have a lot more money than I had in the past—that is, I sort of do, but I sort of don't have that money, it's complicated—but here is what I do have and it is material. I know how to grow food to some degree, how to build a shelter for $50 that is luxurious, and truly sustainable too, not greenwashing. I can survive and thrive without compromising my values and am moving toward that. I have the willingness to do a self-inventory on MY terms, not on ones that I think are Everyone Else's terms. I no longer really believe for long that I need someone or something outside myself to change for me to have contentment and even happiness, even ecstasy.

As an underearner and under be-er who hides out from the world (Editors' note: *UA Symptom 8 Isolation: We choose to work alone when it might serve us much better to have coworkers, associates or employees.*), I now have a relationship-building instrument in my life. The instrument, again, is not something that I was looking for, but something that Higher Power brought to me in the strangest way. In a way, it's been more life-changing than either the spiritual path I said was most pivotal before, or the life-changing professional training which Higher Power paid for on my behalf. It allows me to bring the principles, the essence of sponsoring and of that professional training, into my relationships with other human beings, in a free-from-money dynamic. It promises to become an entire way of life for me, or a set of training wheels that lets me really live that way of life solidly. It feels like an adaptive aid for me personally, perfectly designed to make me coherent. I trust there is another miracle of even greater size on its way, though I have no clue what it might be.

It was only some years after I got through all the Steps, and the professional training, that I got clear about the true nature of my moral inventory, of my impact on the world, other humans, and life around me. (Editors' note: *Step 4: Made a searching and fearless moral inventory of ourselves.*) And with that, solutions came for how I could reduce that negative impact and even put it "in the black" ethically. The willingness to do inventory came through my seeking of community and fellowship, although it didn't happen to be with fellow UA's. The principles of the program were helping me. Keeping the focus on myself as far as acting on the knowledge once I had it, rather than over-depending on that community or human powers, allowed me to begin to make measurable progress. It is two years of inventory now, imperfect but giving solid indication of progress.

Today, I solidly believe my new idea of prosperity is right for me. It would not be appealing to many—"one person's treasure is another person's trash"—but it is ethical, it is one in which I am free to live by my values and in my joy. I may not get to the top of that particular mountain, but I have seen it now. One of the paradoxes of UA is that we're recovering from something no one wants. Lots of people want to drink, to have excessive sex, to spend beyond their means—but not a lot of people want to earn less than what they produce value for. Yet in recovering from this self-starvation, we also don't simply want to make the most money possible at the expense of all other priorities or become powerful at others' expense. Recovery in UA for me is a bit more nuanced than what it might sound like to an outside observer [or to the newcomer]—but I feel wealthy beyond measure.

My recovery is different, my conception and experience of Higher Power is different, from what I think I hear often. But I want more people with more different conceptions of Higher Power to know that they can recover and feel welcome in our Fellowship.

I have to complain of too many life-changing, "mountain top" experiences. I polish over here, and it never shines in the realm of money--well, that's not quite true, it has shone in that area too, sort of, but not so much in earnings. But boy, has it shone. And shone and shone and shone. While it is not the recovery I thought I needed, nor an easily articulable soundbite, it is a clear path forward, and some clear mysteries.

A path that just feels right on the inside, an inner world of freedom and joy.

This story, reprinted from a forthcoming book of program literature for Underearners Anonymous, with permission from the author, who is an anonymous member of that Twelve Step program's fellowship. The reprinting of this story does not imply endorsement of Moving Beyond Money nor lending the name of Underearners Anonymous or Twelve Step fellowships in general to this enterprise. The author does not speak for any Twelve Step program as a whole, nor for Twelve Step fellowships in general. No financing of [name of publication]] has taken place either in money or in kind—neither in gift of money nor of value—and no money has been charged or may be charged by [name of publication] or any other entity for this chapter of the book; the cost of any book containing this chapter has not been increased proportionally for the addition of this story but the chapter is being given as an addition, at cost. The author receives no royalty, and neither *Moving Beyond Money* nor any related causes receive any money from the author or from any Twelve Step fellowship. No modifications may be made to any part of the story, other than language translation or typographic or grammatical corrections, and any annotations (comments) must be clearly marked as such, as being non-attributable to the author. This story may be further reprinted under the same terms with this entire statement by anyone who wishes. Thank you for helping the author honor the principles of the Twelve Traditions of Underearners Anonymous, and for making the message available to all.

—An Anonymous Member of Underearners Anonymous

RESOURCES

The Twelve Steps of Underearners Anonymous

1. We admitted we were powerless over underearning — that our lives had become unmanageable.

2. Came to believe that a Power greater than ourselves could restore us to sanity.

3. Made a decision to turn our will and our lives over to the care of God as we understood God.

4. Made a searching and fearless moral inventory of ourselves.

5. Admitted to God, to ourselves, and to another human being the exact nature of our wrongs.

6. Were entirely ready to have God remove all these defects of character.

7. Humbly asked God to remove our shortcomings.

8. Made a list of all persons we had harmed and became willing to make amends to them all.

9. Made direct amends to such people wherever possible, except when to do so would injure them or others.

10. Continued to take personal inventory and when we were wrong promptly admitted it.

11. Sought through prayer and meditation to improve our conscious contact with God as we understood God, praying only for knowledge of God's will for us and the power to carry that out.

12. Having had a spiritual awakening as the result of these steps, we tried to carry this message to compulsive underearners, and to practice these principles in all our affairs.

The Twelve Traditions of Underearners Anonymous

1. Our common welfare should come first; personal recovery depends upon UA unity.

2. For our group purpose there is but one ultimate authority — a loving God as is expressed in our group conscience. Our leaders are but trusted servants, they do not govern.

3. The only requirement for UA membership is a desire to stop underearning

4. Each group should be autonomous except in matters affecting other groups or UA as a whole.

5. Each group has but one primary purpose — to carry the message to the underearner who still suffers.

6. A UA group ought never endorse, finance, or lend the UA name to any related facility or outside enterprise, lest problems of money, property, or prestige divert us from our primary purpose.

7. Every UA group ought to be fully self-supporting, declining outside contributions.

8. Underearners Anonymous should remain forever non-professional, but our service centers may employ special workers.

9. UA, as such, ought never be organized, but we may create service boards or committees directly responsible to those they serve.

10. Underearners Anonymous has no opinion on outside issues; hence the UA name ought never be drawn into public controversy.

11. Our public relations policy is based on attraction rather than promotion; we need always maintain personal anonymity at the level of press, radio, and films.

12. Anonymity is the spiritual foundation of all our traditions, ever reminding us to place principles before personalities.

12 Signs of Recovery from Underearning

(The UA Symptoms in Reverse)

1. **Time Reverence** - We value and wisely use our time. We use it to accomplish our goals and visions. We quickly do what must be done.

2. **Idea Discernment** -We carefully consider others' ideas. We accept those that make sense for us (i.e., those that get results, and which fit our personalities and circumstances).

3. **Confidence in our Abilities** - Once we have demonstrated competence in our jobs or business, we can calmly communicate our worth and value. We let our results speak for themselves.

4. **Having Only Valuable Possessions** - We have only possessions that serve us, either now or in the future. We may not have a lot, but what we have is of good quality and is clean. We sell, give away or discard that which we no longer need.

5. **Consistency of Effort** - We work consistently with plenty of time for relaxation. We keep a good balance between work and relaxation so that we don't exhaust ourselves nor put off important tasks. We make consistent progress, day by day.

6. **Appropriate Giving Away of Our Time** - We only give away our time when we can easily afford to or when there is a clear benefit to us. Although we are helpful, we don't do it at our expense.

7. **Fair Valuing and Fair Pricing** - We fairly value our abilities and services based on our ability to add value and what the market will bear. We ask for increases in compensation when we deserve it or because the market will bear it. We charge enough so that we can live comfortably while meeting all of our expenses, along with having a surplus for fun, savings, a prudent reserve, and long-term expenses such as retirement.

8. **Fellowship** - We choose to work with others when appropriate, and we work alone when appropriate. We socialize, but not at the expense of time that we need to be by ourselves, whether for rest, planning or work.

9. **Vibrant Health and Energy** - Because we know that we have value, we approach each endeavor with vibrant energy and health.

10. **Feelings of Worthiness** - We feel relaxed when asking for or being given what we need or what we are owed. We realize we are simply asking for that which is rightfully ours.

11. **Follow Through or Completion** - We follow up on opportunities, leads, or jobs that could be profitable. We follow up when it makes sense. We complete projects and tasks except when it doesn't make sense to complete them. Further, because we value our time, we don't complete them at an unnecessary level- i.e., we accept that often things don't need to be done perfectly or sometimes even well. We focus on that which is most relevant to us.

12. **Stability Valuing** - As we realize that stability is an important foundation of our lives, we avoid unnecessary conflict with co-workers, supervisors, and clients. Instead, we build up and validate those around us, resulting in financial prosperity for all.

Resourced from https://www.norcalda.org/underearning 07/2018

Signs of Underearning and Recovery Affirmations

DA's Sign of Compulsively Underearning

- ☐ Resenting low pay or a bad job situation, yet not asking for a raise or changing jobs.
- ☐ Feeling inadequate to perform a job well, while secretly feeling superior to others
- ☐ Believing your salary is not important, yet worrying about money constantly
- ☐ Feeling too discouraged to apply for a job ("I won't get it anyway, and if I do, I'll hate it.")
- ☐ Having trouble finding resumes or job notices in piles of bills or unopened mail
- ☐ Feeling ashamed of your work history and sick with anxiety over job interviews
- ☐ Stealing from employers because you believe they owe you more than they pay you.
- ☐ Spending hours daydreaming but not even minutes working toward your dreams.
- ☐ Overcommitting time and energy to volunteer activities
- ☐ Overworking -- spending hours to do a job more perfectly than you are getting paid to do
- ☐ Being too fearful of failure to get any more training or attempt a new career
- ☐ Believing no one will pay you for anything you enjoy doing

DA's Sign of Recovery from Compulsively Underearning Affirmations

- ☐ I take action daily toward achieving a better paying, more satisfying career.
- ☐ I am pleased with my level of performance and see my work, and the work of those around me, as all equally important.
- ☐ I believe that earning more money is an important and worthwhile goal, so I will always have enough to live and thrive on.
- ☐ When applying for a job, I act as if I will be working there soon and totally loving my new job, and if I don't get hired, it's their loss.
- ☐ I maintain an organized system for filing and following up on important papers, so I can easily locate whatever I need that will help me reach my financial goals and responsibilities on time.
- ☐ Even if my work history is less than perfect, I am prepared and confident in handling, successfully, all kinds of job interview questions. I know how to overcome all objections by emphasizing my assets, of which there are many.
- ☐ I pride myself in keeping a spotless reputation, always focused on giving my best work, even if it goes unnoticed.
- ☐ I write down all my dreams for the future and set aside at least an hour a day toward making them come true.
- ☐ I keep track of how much time I spend volunteering my services for free, and when it is too much, I either cut back or start charging for my time.
- ☐ I plan my assignments responsibly, so that I only spend a reasonable amount of time on them, knowing that the outcome will be "good enough."

- ☐ I am no longer afraid of failure, but rather respond with gratitude to every opportunity for advancing my career by learning something new each day.
- ☐ I know that I will always work my best at what I enjoy doing for others, and others are therefore willing to compensate me well for my area of giftedness.

Vision of Earning Wellness and Wholeness

[3]With the help of our Higher Power as our new employer, the following promises are manifested in our lives:

1. We do what must be done promptly, and we consistently use our time to support our vision and further our goals.

2. We are drawn to and quickly embrace ideas that expand our life and career and that increase our profitability.

3. We act from our consciousness of our true value and worth.

4. We release possessions that no longer serve us thus staying in the prosperous flow.

5. We work in a balanced, consistent, self- loving way.

6. We choose actions and commitments that benefit us and contribute to our prosperity.

7. We request and receive increases in compensation and also what the market will bear.

8. We work with others whenever having co- workers, associates or employees serves us.

9. We experience the physical vitality and health that supports our self-expression and expansion.

---

[3] This text is drawn from the text of the "UA Sample Action Partner Format" (a template on the UA website for a round-robin action group), and was reviewed and approved by the Literature Committee on June 6, 2015; it is proposed to the GSB for approval to become a stand-alone piece of literature on the website and in print; If it is approved by the GSB, then it will be presented to the World Service Conference for final review and approval.

10. We feel at ease and even joyful when asking for or being given what we need or what we are owed.

11. We follow up on opportunities, leads, or jobs that could be profitable. We complete projects and tasks that we begin.

12. We work harmoniously and in a spirit of service with co-workers, supervisors, and clients, generating good will that results in ever-greater financial prosperity.

Big Book 10th Step Nightly Review Questions[4]

Was I resentful?

Was I selfish?

Was I dishonest?

Was I afraid?

Do I owe an apology?

Have I kept something to myself which should be discussed with another person at once?

Was I kind and loving toward all?

What could I have done better?

Was I thinking of myself most of the time?

Was I thinking of what I could do for others, of what I could pack into the stream of life?

---

[4] These questions are sourced from the Big Book of AA nightly review as suggested on page 86 of the 2001 volume.

How to Run a Writers' Goals Group[5]

1. **Schedule** at least an hour. With five people, we scheduled 75 minutes per week. With four, we are often content with an hour. FYI, the members of our group all live in different places. We have never had a face-to-face Goals Group meeting. Before the pandemic, we met over a free phone conference line. We then switched to video conference.

2. **Start** with the Serenity Prayer, "we" version.

3. One group member chairs, the second member keeps time.

4. **Write** for 10 minutes on a prompt:
   To find a prompt, we started by taking one question or short section after another from the UA literature tab's "Goals Pages." We have also gone through the piece titled "Underearning and Thinking," briefly used the "Visions-Goals-Actions Worksheet," and have returned to the Goals Pages in a more haphazard way, with the chair choosing which ever question or small section speaks to them at the moment.

5. Each group member **reads their writing** aloud. No feedback. No time constraint.

6. **Divide** the remaining time by the people present, setting aside five minutes at the end for any group business and closing prayer.

7. **Shares** go in the same order in which members shared their writing on the prompt. Each member tells the time-keeper when they want warnings and how much time they want to reserve for feedback, then shares their progress toward their vision(s) and goals in the time allotted.

---

[5] This was contributed by Felicia; see her chapter where she describes how the process worked for her recovery.

8. Other group members **offer feedback** in time reserved for that, sharing "popcorn style," i.e., as the spirit moves. They try to be conscious of limited time and to allow for each member to offer some feedback.

9. **Ending**: Consideration of any business, for example scheduling of future meetings, any anticipated absences of group members, ideas for sprucing up format, or stray thoughts that come up after having listened to everyone's shares.

10. **Close** with another "we" version of Serenity Prayer, ending "Thy will, not ours, be done."

Made in United States
Troutdale, OR
11/03/2026

56847565R00066